Medical Law
& Ethics

Michel Lipman

REGENTS/PRENTICE HALL
UPPER SADDLE RIVER, NEW JERSEY 07458

Lipman, Michel, 1913-
   Medical law and ethics / Michel Lipman.
     p. cm.
   Includes index.
   ISBN 0-13-064585-0
   1. Medical laws and legislation--United States. 2. Medical
ethics--United States.   I. Title.
   [DNLM: 1. Legislation, Medical--United States. 2. Jurisprudence--
United States. 3. Ethics, Medical--United States. W 32.5 AA1
L76m 1994]
KF3821.L57 1994
174'.2--dc20
DNLM/DLC
for Library of Congress   93-1344
                                 CIP

Editorial/production supervision
  and interior design: *Cathy Frank*
Cover design: *Dana Boll*
Prepress Buyer: *Ilene Sanford*
Manufacturing Buyer: *Ed O'Dougherty*
Acquisitions Editor: *Mark Hartman*
Editorial Assistant: *Louise Fullam*

 © 1994 by REGENTS/PRENTICE HALL
A Division of Simon & Schuster
Upper Saddle River, New Jersey 07458

Printed in the United States of America

10 9 8 7 6 5 4 3 2

ISBN 0-13-064585-0

PRENTICE-HALL INTERNATIONAL (UK) LIMITED, *London*
PRENTICE-HALL OF AUSTRALIA PTY. LIMITED, *Sydney*
PRENTICE-HALL CANADA INC., *Toronto*
PRENTICE-HALL HISPANOAMERICANA, S.A., *Mexico*
PRENTICE-HALL OF INDIA PRIVATE LIMITED, *New Delhi*
PRENTICE-HALL OF JAPAN, INC., *Tokyo*
SIMON & SCHUSTER ASIA PTE. LTD., *Singapore*
EDITORA PRENTICE-HALL DO BRASIL, LTDA., *Rio de Janeiro*

For Myriam
Beloved friend

Contents

INDEX

Preface

Today's health providers have a history so ancient that its beginnings are lost in the clouds of time. Homer, who wrote eight centuries before Christ, wrote of the skill of some warriors to treat wounds and perform surgery. He also mentions Asclepius, a Thessalian king and his sons Machaon and Podalirius; these early professionals were said to treat not only injuries, but could recognize "what was not visible to the eye, and tend what could not be healed."

But we can guess that medicine of a kind was practiced far earlier than that—perhaps 30,000 years, to the time of the cave drawings. These drawings show a great amount of accurate observation; it's likely that people so observing would also know something of the healing powers of herbs and natural pharmaceuticals. Even today, among some very primitive tribes, there are "wise women" who assist at birth and attend the sick, using botanicals from the forests around them.

It was Hippocrates who laid the cornerstone for medical practice that was to follow him. Rightly called the "Father of Medicine," he condemned the superstitions and magical charms and amulets of the day. He seems to have studied case-books (charts?) of patients in asclepia, and to have concluded that diseases must be scientifically treated as subject to natural laws. And he powerfully influenced the direction of those who followed him.

Even more important, was Hippocrates' recognition that the physician owed something more than a cure to the man or woman whose life was in his hands. He insisted that the patient's benefit come first, that healing must be the physician's sole aim. And he demands behavior that was not necessarily recognized by the laws of the time: the physician will not voluntarily corrupt or seduce his patients. And he will invoke a special confidentiality: "Whatever I see in the life of men which ought not to be spoken abroad, I will not divulge." And to this very day, the patient may reveal his or her deepest secrets in reliance on the physician's oath of silence.

The point is that Hippocrates demanded special conduct of physicians that lay people were not subject to. This is the concept of *professional ethics*; behavior that is not usually mandated by law. The punishment for violation had nothing to do with courts; it was that a physician no longer be respected but that the reverse be his lot. In other words, professional death with dishonor. A fate not unlike those provided today by medical licensing boards.

The concept of ethical conduct has been extended to health disciplines other than doctors or medicine. It applies to registered nurses, to other licensed nurses, to therapists, technicians, technologists, pharmacists, and other professionals dealing with users of medical services. Many of these disciplines have developed codes of ethical conduct that differ from the physicians' oath. But basically they provide a broad statement of the members' responsibilities and duties as professional people.

Over the years, the fine lines between law and ethics have become blurred. In some states, for example, there are laws which confirm the obligation (or *right?*) of professionals such as physicians, licensed nurses, lawyers, and ministers, to treat patients' disclosures as confidential. But at the same time, the laws permit psychotherapists, for instance, to disclose to a psychotic's intended victim that the person is loose and may do harm.

Medical Law and Ethics discusses both subjects as one, and in related context. Also, the material covered is not for physicians alone. There are important interrelationships between physicians, health centers, rest home operators, technicians, nurses, and other skilled employees and providers. An injudicious act by any one may have serious repercussions on another, in addition to the patients. For, in some situations, patient safety may be at stake, where an individual practitioner or group may have to take action as a matter of conscience. As, for example, where a facility reduces staffing to dangerous levels.

With a better understanding of the legal obligations of each discipline, the members of one can often be helpful to those in another. For instance, it is the physician's obligation to inform the patient and obtain consent to major procedures. If a nurse notes that a patient has not been so informed, he or she, knowing of the obligation, will bring it to the physician's attention. This could very well defuse a potentially dangerous situation.

Much of the material appearing here resulted from my several exciting and happy years as corporate counsel for the California Nurses Association. Among those wonderfully dedicated people were association president Rheba de Tornay, executive director Lionne Conta, former legal counsel Grace Barbee, archivist Margaret McMurray, field representative Florence Terrazzas, and scores of others in that organization whose patience and thoughtful information were wonderfully helpful; to them all, my sincere thanks and appreciation.

Ethics is a kind of moral law

Introduction

One of the marks of an advanced society is the level of ethics of its professions. Ethics is a kind of *moral* law. It differs from what we may call written law—which we get from judges and our legislators. Yet ethics and law are both guidelines to behavior, and often overlap.

For example, the law prohibits physicians from divulging the secrets of patients even in the courtroom. But for centuries before such laws, physicians swore Hippocrates' oath, which says, in part: "*[W]hatsoever I shall see or hear of the lives of men which is not fitting to be spoken, I will keep inviolably secret....*"

The Hippocratic oath is the foundation for today's medical ethics, which apply not only to physicians but also to registered nurses, therapists, psychologists, aides, secretaries, and others involved directly or indirectly with patient care. Other professions have developed their own codes of ethics, including lawyers, judges, clergy, accountants, and others. "The greatness of man consists in saying what is true, and in acting according to nature," said Heraclitis, a philosopher who lived around 500 B.C. The great Roman statesman Cicero (106–43 B.C.) wrote, "The safety of the people shall be the highest law." In our own day, Albert Camus said, "I note every day that integrity has no need of rules."

Although the professions do need laws and rules, perhaps the most understandable and simple approach is to act according to what you know in your heart to be right. But even that definition is not perfect. A medical professional may truly and honestly believe that in a particularly tragic case it would be humane and charitable to administer euthanasia, but the law prohibits that completely. The lethal pill or injection is homicide, and the person involved may be subject to criminal penalties.

In dealing with human life, there are sometimes excruciating dilemmas. Many have too precise or comfortable answers. Yet, as a medical professional, you may sooner or later be forced to make such difficult decisions. This book cannot make those decisions for you. It can only describe some of the major decisions and tell you what courts and lawmakers have done about them. Those laws and decisions may act as guidelines, but there are times when the solution is "off the map" and you must, on the basis of your own sense of humanity and good judgment, make up your own mind.

Even there, you might not find the ideal answer. If your act transcends the ethical rules of your profession, you may not have broken a law. But you could be expelled or suspended from your professional association, your license could be suspended or revoked, or you could justifiably be discharged by your employer.

With all of this, there is no need to be intimidated by the moral, ethical, or legal problems that may develop in your career. You might well have comparable problems in other vocations as well. In medicine, because we set such a high value on life and health, we accordingly set high standards of conduct for those who work in this exacting field.

You may take commendable pride in the fact that the standards are high and that you have been willing to accept the discipline, study, and hard work needed to become a significant part of this profession. *Pax vobiscum!*

MML September 1, 1992

1

The Practitioner's Parachute

Who tells the patient about the risks of surgery?

∎

When does the patient give his or her consent to a procedure?

∎

Does a patient lose all rights to sue for malpractice by signing a consent form?

∎

Must a consent form be witnessed?

∎

Is it illegal to operate without a signed, witnessed consent form?

A patient can't be a patient unless she consents. Does that sound absurd? A man walks into a physician's office with a bad cold. "Godda stubbed up nose, Doc. Bad cough, too." The doctor takes the man's pulse, looks down his throat, auscultates his chest. "Get some rest, lots of fluids, two aspirins three times a day. And I'll give you a prescription for that cough."

Now the ancient law, which is still in effect, gives each of us control over who shall so much as touch us. For centuries, the law has held the individual inviolable. It protects us from unpermitted and unprivileged contact of any kind. How? By making it a crime to touch anyone intentionally without consent. Technically, such touching is *battery* (оскорбление действием)

So hasn't our physician committed battery? He touched the patient during the examination, didn't he? So why isn't he a lawbreaker 20, 30, 50 times a day, depending on the number of patients he sees? Because the patients *consent* to the touching. In writing? No. In spoken words? No; the patient consents through *action*. Mary Jones comes into the office with a complaint—just about any complaint—*knowing* that there'll be minor touching at some point of the examination and perhaps an injection, cauterization, or other procedure.

[kɔ:tərai'zeiʃən] прижигание

CONSENT BY IMPLICATION

There's no crime here because by coming to the office and giving her reason, *she consents by implication.* As a reasonably intelligent person, she knows in a general way what to expect. The law does not say that she must announce in advance, "Doctor, I hereby consent to have my temperature taken." That would be absurd; of course.

"Consent by implication" also applies to medical workers other than the physician. If you work in a doctor's office, a hospital, a nursing home, or other medical facility, you do not need written consent for your actions. You must, of course, be acting within the scope of your job, whether it be taking a blood sample, turning a patient in bed, or walking a patient.

Suppose that a man is injured in an accident and is brought to a medical facility in an unconscious state. He plainly isn't capable of making decisions regarding his condition. If possible, the consent should come from a relative or close friend. But very often this is not possible. The injury may require immediate attention, perhaps major surgery. The rule is that in an *emergency*, medical people may do many things that might otherwise not be proper. As long as they act within the limits of good practice consistent with the conditions, they need not worry over lack of consent.

The same is true if you happen to be present at, say, a train wreck or highway pileup. If you have some training, even if you're not an M.D. or R.N., and if there is no other medical help present, you may take action to help the injured. You will not be held responsible for what you did if what you did is what anyone else with your level of training would reasonably do under those circumstances. On the other hand, you aren't compelled by law to do anything—no matter what your degree of training.

WHEN WRITTEN CONSENT IS NEEDED

As we've seen, there's no need for a written consent form for most medical visits involving only examination and minor treatment. The problems start when the patient doesn't know—or can't be expected to know—the dangers in the more-than-minor procedures. Now the tough questions arise. First, who tells the patient what the procedure is all about and what the dangers might be?

Here's Dr. Emerson, running almost two hours behind schedule and the waiting room still full of patients. She says to her registered nurse, "Mary, will you explain to Mrs. Hoskins what her surgery is and have her sign the consent form?" Mary, an experienced and competent professional, does exactly what the physician asked. She tells Mrs. Hoskins about the anesthesia she'll receive, just where they'll cut into her back, and what they'll do to her troublesome spine. "You'll get a mild tranquilizer beforehand so that you won't feel tense and nervous. You won't feel any pain at all. Afterward, there'll be some discomfort, but don't worry about that. You'll get medication that will help you."

Mrs. Hoskins twists her handkerchief. "It's not—I mean, there is some danger, isn't there? I've got a daughter in high school...."

"I understand, Mrs. Hoskins. Now don't worry. Dr. Emerson is a marvelous surgeon. Of course there's always some danger in any surgery. Possible infection. A damaged nerve. Or the healing might not take place normally. But those things are rare. There's no reason why your surgery shouldn't turn out just fine." The patient sighs. "Well, if you say so...." And she signs the form that Mary holds out to her.

Unfortunately, the surgery does not help Mrs. Hoskins. In fact, her condition becomes worse. She sues the doctor. Why should she do that? Wasn't she warned there were possible dangers? Didn't she sign an informed consent form? Yes and no. She wasn't *fully* informed. There were, it seems, alternative kinds of treatment that she wasn't told about—perhaps not as effective as the surgery might have been, perhaps with a lower relief rate. But the patient *should have been allowed to make the choice herself.* And on *that* basis, she could have the consent form set aside and go ahead with her lawsuit.

There's another point here against the physician. She should have informed the patient herself. It is the physician who knows the patient and on whose judgment the patient relies. *The physician cannot delegate so important a task to anyone else except under emergency conditions.* He or she may run videotaped information for the patient or give the patient literature about the condition. But at some point the physician must discuss it personally and make sure that the patient is fully aware of the procedure, the possible dangers, and the possible alternatives.

BUT PERHAPS NOT EVERYTHING...

Patients come in all shapes, sizes, ages, and conditions. The patient who is alert, feels good, and is functioning well may be better able to understand the physician's explanation quickly and easily, without becoming "unglued." But many patients are not so fortunate.

Some may be elderly, some mentally impaired, some acutely ill, some nervous and excitable, possibly to the point where full disclosure may lead to profound shock. The physician must then use good professional judgment. It has been said that "if, in the judgment of the attending physician, the patient is not considered to be of sound mind, or mentally competent...if he is under the influence of drugs or alcohol, the initial or continuing consent should be given by his legal representatives." That would be a spouse, guardian, or in the case of a minor, usually the parents.

What, though, if the patient *is* fully competent but in so unfortunate a state of health that one more shock would be a real hazard? What if the medical professionals actually do withhold information about the risks?

That was the question in a case where the patient had a serious heart condition that required prompt surgery. The patient was already suffering from more than one serious ailment. The physician felt that news of one more strike against him would greatly impair his chances of recovery. The patient was already in an acute nervous state.

Cautiously, the physician explained that there would have to be surgery to correct a suspected aneurysm. He did not, however, mention that the operation could possibly cause paralysis. Thus when the patient signed the release, he was not fully informed. Unfortunately, the operation did result in paralysis, and the patient sued, claiming that he should have been told of the risk and given the opportunity to choose whatever other alternatives there were. The court rejected the patient's argument. It said that under these particular circumstances, the physician was justified in keeping information about the danger from him.

This is as good a rule as can be found: that the withholding of risk information may be permitted under special circumstances. As a further protection, the physician should consider revealing the entire story to a family member or spouse and making it clear to that person that the deliberate withholding is due to concern for the patient's condition.

ROLE OF THE MEDICAL ASSISTANT

The medical assistant can play an important role in the preoperative stage of treatment. Let's assume that you are working in a hospital setting. The patient is in his room, with surgery scheduled for the following morning. The patient seems restless and tense and asks a lot of questions. Some of them are related to the surgery he is facing.

You're worried about this. You know patients sometimes ask questions mainly for reassurance—but this is different; the man really doesn't seem to know what he's there for. Wisely, you go to your supervisor and tell your concern.

"It's good you brought that up," the supervisor tells you. "Let's take a look at the chart and make sure that there's a consent form on file." Together, you look at the chart. And sure enough, there is a signed consent form, as hospital policy requires. Your supervisor says, "This protects the hospital. But I don't see anything here that protects the doctor. Maybe we'd better check with him."

When the doctor hears what you say, he rubs his chin. "To tell the truth, I can't remember if I discussed the surgery with him or not. I'll go see him right away and do so." A little while later the doctor drops by the office where you are working. There's a slightly embarrassed smile on his face. "Thanks very much for reminding me. I had a talk with our patient, told him the risks and alternatives, and he said he felt much better. He wants to go ahead with the surgery, and has signed a consent form for me to handle it."

That case had a happy ending. But if the doctor had not been reminded to get the release, and if there had been unmentioned complications, he could very well have lost a lawsuit. This is true no matter how skillfully the doctor has performed the surgery. This kind of suit is not for malpractice—that occurs when a physician does not treat a patient according to prevailing standards. It is a suit based on failure to furnish full information, for depriving a patient of his right to choose alternatives. He may always choose not to have the surgery at all—which may be an unwise choice. But it is his right to make that choice if he wishes to—and it is a right that the courts will carefully enforce.

The medical assistant can be of valuable help in any case involving surgery by checking to make sure that there is signed informed consent both for the *physician* and for the *hospital.* Sometimes the two consents may be merged into one form. In either case you should mention this to the appropriate party if either one is not covered.

Generally, consent forms are signed after the surgical patient's workup. By that time the physician should have had time to make a final diagnosis and explain to the patient what must be done, and the risks involved, and answer any questions that remain.

WHAT'S IN THAT ALL-IMPORTANT FORM

To the surgical patient, the surgical staff's job is relatively easy. They've discovered something wrong with his interior mechanism, and they fix it by taking something out, adding something, or a little of both. Actually, the surgical peoples' responsibilities go far beyond cutting and stitching. There are a number of relationships of which the patient is not even aware, such as supervised medical students, unnamed and unknown nurses and an anesthetist or two. And there are understandings that need to be clearly expressed and agreed to.

A typical consent form will cover the following subjects (though usually in more extended language):

1. Authorization to a particular physician to perform a particular operation, and authority to perform any *other* procedures that might be advisable. (For example, the operation may be to resection a bowel, and the surgeon discovers an inflamed appendix as well.)
2. Agreement on a particular surgeon with the possible addition of staff doctors, residents, and medical students. Also the possibility that other licensed physicians, including residents, may perform part of the surgery under that surgeon's supervision.
3. The patient acknowledges that he or she has been told the purpose and nature of the treatment, the risks, and the possible complications. The patient acknowledges that no one has guaranteed the results.
4. The patient agrees to accept anesthesia, with named exceptions, if any.
5. The patient agrees that he or she knows that sterility may result (if there is, in fact, such a possibility).

6. Patient agrees to the disposal of tissue or organ parts removed, with whatever exceptions there may be.

7. The patient consents to photographs or televising of the surgery for medical, scientific, or education purposes, or for publication, without identification of the patient.

8. There may also be a consent for qualified observers (such as medical students, nurses, trainees) to be present during the surgery.

9. The patient further consents to being observed and examined by medical students during convalescence.

10. Patient certifies to having read, and fully understands the explanations made to him, and that appropriate changes were made in the printed consent before signing.

11. The patient might or might not wish to state his or her religion.

This is followed by spaces for signatures. If the patient is a minor or is unable to sign, there is space for the signature of closest relative or guardian.

Wording will vary in various facilities. Forms used for outpatient surgery will generally be shorter and less formal. Often the forms used will have a number of paragraphs that don't apply to the particular case. These should be ruled out with a pen and initialed by both the patient and the physician.

If the patient has a particular request, it can be written in and also initialed, if agreeable to both parties. For example, a pregnant woman might want a tubal ligation (sterilization) after her baby is born—but only if the baby is healthy and normal. That condition in the consent form may be very important to her, and it will give her a sense of security knowing that it's there (as well as being good medical–legal practice).

Farfetched? Not really. A prominent trial lawyer says that if that physician became absentminded and did the tubal ligation although the child is obviously deformed, he can and probably should be sued. Putting it in writing, therefore, is a good way of reminding him what he is limited to.

PARACHUTES DON'T ALWAYS OPEN

How protective is a signed informed consent? The doctor has explained, the patient has signed, but the treatment doesn't turn out as well as expected. Is the patient forever barred from filing suit? Generally, yes—*but not always*. Take the hypothetical case of a surgeon discussing a proposed thyroidectomy. "There's a very good chance, Mrs. Grayson, that it will improve your condition—better than 80 percent, I'd say. But it's also possible it may not help you at all—that's around a 10 to 12 percent chance. So you understand, don't you, that there's no guarantee?"

Mrs. Grayson smiles. "That's better odds than I'd get at most horse races," she says. "How soon can we do it?" She signs the informed consent, and the surgery is done. Unfortunately, she doesn't improve; in fact, her condition gets worse.

Does she have a claim against the doctor? Yes. Despite her signature, she can sue. Of course, the doctor's lawyer will exclaim, "But she *was* informed! The doctor very clearly told her the surgery might not help her at all. He *said* there was no guarantee!" "Very true," Mrs. Grayson's counsel says. "He said she might not get better. But he *failed* to tell her that she might get *worse*! So she had no way of coming to a truly informed decision!" And there's no doubt the court would rule in favor of Mrs. Grayson.

Physicians should understand that when the courts say that consents should be informed, they mean *fully* informed of every material risk and danger. As a medical assistant, you won't always be present at such discussions. But suppose that you know the doctor you work for is apt to be happily optimistic, and you know that a particular patient is inclined to be difficult. You just might say, tactfully, "I wonder, doctor, how Mr. Appleby will react when you tell him there's a chance the surgery may make him worse?" A gentle reminder at the right time might really save the day!

What if there is some reason that the patient *cannot* be informed? A man is brought into surgery unconscious and badly mangled from an auto accident. The man cannot respond to questions. There's no relative or friend who can be reached in time. The surgeon performs immediate surgery, giving the patient three units of blood during the procedure, and saves his life.

Later, when the patient is conscious, he asks, "You didn't give me blood, did you?" And when told that the surgeon had done so, he becomes very distraught. He is a devout member of a religious organization which believes that transfusions are contrary to the laws of God. He claims that he would rather have died than accept human blood into his veins.

Can he sue the surgeon? No. There was no way the surgeon could have known how the patient felt about transfusions. She acted, and acted promptly, to save a life, and the law will certainly not penalize her for that. Parenthetically, it might well be that people who do not want certain medical procedures under any circumstances should and sometimes do wear a medical medallion with that information on it.

A related question: Suppose that parents who hold similar beliefs have a small child who is injured or ill and needs blood, and suppose that the parents refuse to give their consent to its use? Then the medical people can go into court and get a hearing in a matter of hours. They can present the problem, the parents can be heard, and the court will rule whether the child should or should not get blood. In such cases the judge will usually (but not always) rule in favor of the medical people and thus for the administration of blood.

ASSISTANTS' IMPORTANT ROLE

Medical assistants can be of considerable help in "falling between the chairs" situations—where the referring physician assumes that the specialist will give the patient full information, and the specialist assumes that the referring office has done so. A tactful query would have quickly solved this problem in a Connecticut case. The internist diagnosed a patient's ailment as lupus. He advised a kidney biopsy to see how much involvement there was. He said it was a simple procedure and that the patient should leave the hospital in a day or two if there were no complications. He said that the urologist who would perform the biopsy would describe the procedure in more detail.

The urologist explained that this would be done with a needle, and there might be some pain. He did not mention the alternative of an open biopsy, which he did not favor. Nor did he mention that it was possible that the gallbladder might be punctured. The patient signed an informed consent, and the procedure was done. During the procedure, the patient's gallbladder was punctured and had to be removed. She sued the urologist (and others, who were later dismissed).

In defense, the urologist said that he didn't tell the patient about the alternative open biopsy because he had tried them in the past and did not consider them viable alternatives to the needle biopsy. Under those circumstances, did the urologist fulfill his duty to inform the patient under the appropriate standard?

No, he did not, the court ruled, adding that "Every human adult of sound mind has a right to determine what shall be done with his own body, and a surgeon who performs an operation without his patients' consent, commits an assault, for which he is liable in damages." And, it said, "All viable alternatives [must] be disclosed even though some involve more hazards than others."

Every trained medical person involved in the care of patients should be alert to the need to properly inform the patient of risks and alternatives.

GUIDELINES FOR CONSENTS

These suggestions can help you protect physicians and hospital against a lawsuit, and protect the patient against unforeseen and unwanted invasions of his person:

1. *Be sure that there's a signed, dated, and witnessed consent on file a reasonable time before the procedure is done.*
   Comment: You want this to be a *reasonable time* before; otherwise, the patient may claim that he or she was sedated at the time of signing and so was not competent to make the decision.
2. *Notify your supervisor if you believe that the patient was*

sedated at the time of signing and that his or her mental ability and judgment might be affected.

Comment: In such a case the procedure might be deferred until the patient is sufficiently clearheaded to decide. If this is not feasible, the patient's closest relative or a friend might act for the patient.

3. *Raise the question if you think the patient has not been properly informed.*

Comment: If may be that the patient has a poor understanding of English; or the physician may simply have overlooked informing the patient. Or something may have happened to upset the patient's mental state before he or she signed.

4. *Don't try to inform the patient unless you are a physician. This is exclusively a medical function.*

Comment: There have been suggestions that the physician may delegate this duty to a registered nurse or other well-qualified professional. This is doubtful. The person who accepts such an assignment may find himself or herself a defendant in a lawsuit along with the physician.

REFERENCES

Gary v. *Grunnagle*, 223 A.2d 663 (Pa. 1966).

LIPMAN MICHEL M., Informed Consent and the Nurse's Role, *RN Magazine*, September 1972.

Logan v. *Greenwich Hospital Association*, 38 ALR 4, 879.

LUDLAM, JAMES E., *California Hospital Association Consent Manual.*

Negaard v. *Feda's Estate*, 446 P.2d 436 (Mont. 1968).

QUESTIONS

1. A patient visits her physician, pointing out a small growth on her lip. The physician correctly diagnoses the growth as a skin cancer. He tells the patient that he can remove it surgically with very little risk and only a minor scar. He asks her to sign a consent form for the surgery and she does so. The surgery is successful.

A year later, the patient is back. This time she has a growth on the inner lobe of an ear. The physician says that surgery might leave a noticeable deformation of the lobe. He recommends removal with liquid nitrogen and the patient agrees that would be better. However, this procedure is not successful; the cancer spreads and requires extensive surgery. The patient sues for malpractice.

The physician points out that the patient signed a consent form stating specifically that she understood the risks and that the results could not be guaranteed. The patient responds that the consent form she signed was for the *first* procedure only; she never signed a second one, and she was never told the nitrogen process might not remove all the affected tissue.

How do you think this case should be resolved?

2. The patient, a crotchety elderly man, had been prepped and sedated and was ready to be wheeled into surgery. At that very moment, the R.N., who had been reviewing the patient's file, made a discovery. "Doctor," she said, "there's no consent form here!" The doctor was busy. "Well, they're ready there for him in surgery now, and I'll be another moment. As long as the patient is conscious and knows what is happening, have him sign one now." The nurse did as she was told. When presented with a pen and a consent form on a clipboard, the old gentleman snarled "Why not? They'll probably murder me in there anyway." And he signed. The procedure turned out badly, with serious complications. The patient sued.

Should the printed, signed consent protect the physician against the suit? Would your answer be the same if the patient had refused to sign but it was imperative to perform the surgery anyway?

3. The patient had just been bitten by a venomous snake. The physician hurried to the scene. The situation called for fast action, and the physician injected antivenom at the bases of the bitten fingers. She did not mention risks or alternatives. Later, the patient developed gangrene and the fingers had to be amputated. He sued the physician, pointing out that the treatment was contrary to the instructions in the antivenom kit that was used.

What arguments might the patient have used in favor of this claim?

What arguments might the physician have used in her defense?

How do you think the court might have ruled—and why?

2

State of the Chart

Who owns the patient's chart?

∎

Does the government have a right to see a chart without the patient's consent?

∎

Must you let the patient see his or her chart on demand?

∎

When may an employer have information from a patient's chart?

∎

How long must you keep the chart after the patient goes elsewhere?

You're busy at your desk sorting charts to be filed when two well-dressed, clean-cut young men walk in. They show you cards identifying themselves as government investigators. "I wonder if you can help us" one of them says. "My partner and I need to see the chart of Gus Casperson. It will take us but a moment to take a couple of notes. Would you get it for us, please?"

Your heart beats a little faster. *Government? Investigators?* Wow! This is the most exciting thing that's happened all week! You know that the Casperson chart is in the filing cabinet not five feet away. You know that it's supposed to be confidential. But this isn't just *anyone* asking to see it— it's The Law! Surely the CIA or FBI or whoever these gentlemen are must be after an important criminal.

So what do you do? Or say? Say "I'll be glad to tell Dr. Smith you're here, and you can ask him as soon as he's through with his patient." In turn, Dr. Smith should say to them, "Certainly, gentlemen; I'll be glad to have Ms. Jones get it for you if you will let me have the written waiver signed by my patient."

If they do, fine. Give them the chart and a place to sit down and study it. And have someone there to watch and make sure that they take nothing out or add something that wasn't there before. When they've finished, be sure to put the signed waiver in the chart and note the date and time the investigators looked at it. Why? To protect yourself against a charge that you violated the patient's right of privacy.

What if they don't have a waiver signed by the patient? Then the question is, "In that case, gentlemen, do you have a subpoena or a search warrant?" One of the investigators looks insulted. "Doctor, this is just a routine check. I'm sure you want to cooperate with the government and not put us to the trouble and expense of getting a court order." The doctor smiles. "I cooperate with the government every April 15th—and whenever else it's appropriate. But the law prohibits us from divulging anything in anyone's chart except with the patient's consent or on proper order of a court. I'm sure you understand my position." And that should end the matter, unless they come back later with the necessary authority.

To the nonmedical person, the term *chart* suggests a single sheet of information such as a map or special data. However, in the medical office or hospital, the chart is usually a folder containing separate sheets of information about a patient. The chart of a very long term patient may be several inches thick and may be made up of several folders.

In many ways a patient's chart is his or her life history; the person's entire medical biography is there. The chart memorializes, by documentation, the patient's symptoms and history, examination and tests, findings, diagnosis, treatment, and medications. It may contain many different types of documents: among them a record of admission to a hospital, consents to procedures, emergency room record, history and physical examination, physician's admitting notes, and orders (usually in triplicate: one in the chart, one for nurses' records, one for the pharmacy). There'll be laboratory data and special test results: x-ray, EKG, EEG, and nuclear medicine findings. These are only a few of the kinds of notes, memos, and records that may find their way into a chart.

A chart may not always be complete at any given moment. There could be additional information pending in a physician's incomplete file, or the intern file, or the death file, or the tissue committee file. According to Lane, there may be data in the autopsy secretary's file, nursing department office, clerk's basket, or coding specialist's basket.

Plainly, the accumulated charts of patients over a period of time can become a massive library in large health facilities. There have been suggestions that the ubiquitous computer might be used to store these records, and some efforts have been made to try this on an experimental basis. It is said that the chief objection—that of possible errors—can be compensated for by a feedback control. On the other hand, there is a certain reluctance on the part of many health staff people who feel comfortable with the present paper system and might be reluctant to change to a printout for information.

There is also the question of confidentiality. How do you protect patient information against anyone with a terminal, a phone line, and electronic equipment capable of overriding security guards? Further, there is a legal problem, called the "best evidence" rule. This means that you cannot produce a copy of anything in court unless you can show that the original is lost or there is a good reason why it isn't available. There would certainly be a strong objection at this time to a printout of surgery reports, for example, or any other document that is not the original.

With all these questions, it's likely to be quite a few years until today's charts, clumsy though they may be, are replaced by the busy electrons of the flickering screen. It's possible that early users of computers may be physicians who see patients in their own offices and whose records may be more routine in nature. This may also be true of long-term care facilities, where patients are more or less stable and there is little change, or fewer notes, and certainly less complexity.

Who owns those expensive, voluminous, intimate charts? One might guess, with some reason, that the patient does. After all, he or she went to the physician or facility in the first place, and by doing so, authorized the opening of the chart. And the patient paid for it, too—directly, or indirectly through insurance or government agency. But he or she doesn't own it.

Chart ownership has seldom been questioned in court, and when it has, the decision has gone to the physician or hospital. But that ownership carries certain legal responsibilities as well as some ethical duties. Suppose, for example, that Dr. X's patient, Mrs. Y, decides to change physicians. She goes to Dr. Z about a painful lower backache she's had for a long time. Dr. Z wants to see some early x-rays, taken by Dr. X two years before.

Dr. Z calls his colleague. "Dr. X, Mrs. Y has consulted me about her low back pain. I suspect some arthritic involvement, probably long standing. Would you mind sending over your x-rays so I can take a look?" Dr. X responds, "Ordinarily, Dr. Z, I'd be happy to. But unfortunately, Mrs. Y turned out to be a most unpleasant and difficult patient, and I feel no obligation to cooperate with her by furnishing those films. I'm sorry I can't oblige you. Goodbye."

It may be that those early x-rays are not critical to the patient's treatment. But doesn't Dr. X have an obligation to make them available? He probably does not have a legal obligation. But according to a statement of the American

College of Radiology, he does have an *ethical* obligation. Can Dr. Z get help from that organization? Perhaps. But he should first write a letter to Dr. X, mentioning the statement and requesting his compliance, adding that he should not like to bring the matter to the attention of the ACR.

If he does in fact bring it up, he should, of course, be very careful to state only provable facts and not to draw conclusions or inferences. Otherwise, he risks a possible libel suit. There's another possibility. If Mrs. Y is engaged in a law suit, in which her back pain is an issue, or if she is in litigation over a workers' compensation claim, she can have the x-ray subpoenaed. A subpoena is a document, usually signed by the clear of the court, ordering a person to hand over, or bring to court, the documents it describes. If a subpoena were to be served on Dr. X, he would have to turn over the x-rays. Failure to do so could bring stiff penalties—such as fine or imprisonment. Or both.

Actually, there are very few refusals to furnish chart information to other physicians. Some may authorize their office manager or nurse or secretary to send the x-rays or lab reports or a consultant's report to any doctor who phones in. That's where you have to be a bit cautious. Suppose that the inquiring doctor has a bad reputation; he's been sued many times for malpractice, been arrested for being under the influence of alcohol, and there are proceedings pending before a medical licensing board to revoke his license. Suppose that you turn chart information over to this person, who harms the patient through his criminal negligence. It's possible that if you (or anyone else handling charts in the office) knows about this doctor's reputation, you and the physician you work for could be held responsible, too. Although this is an unusual situation, be sure to check with your employer if you have an inkling of anything along this line. Your employer may, in turn, want to check with his or her attorney.

Let's look at another situation that is not unusual. You get a call from Dr. Johnson, whom you do not know. A former patient of your office is seeing him for a sprained arm. "I'd very much appreciate seeing the films you took of his left shoulder about six months ago. By the way, I'm a doctor of chiropractic." Some states license doctors of chiropractic

(D.C.s), and in fact, there is considerable cooperation now between the members of these respective professions. Licensed D.C.s may use massage, adjustments, and other manipulations, and some who have specialized have been very helpful in long-term osteopathic therapy and rehabilitation. In those cases you may safely (with your employer's approval) turn over records or make them available for review.

A word of caution. What if the chiropractor (or other nonmedical health practitioner) is *not* licensed? Or if licensed, does not enjoy a good reputation? In that case, play it safe. Do not give out the information or records—not even at the request of the patient.

There is some legal opinion—a minority, to be sure—which says that *you* may be at fault if you turn over the records, and the chiropractor harms the patient through gross negligence, based on his or her interpretation of those records. Farfetched, possibly, but consider the arguments. The attorney for the suing patient tells the court, "Your Honor, this patient's chart is a highly technical and difficult-to-understand history of an illness. The physician should have known that a person of lesser medical skills might easily misinterpret the material and by relying on that misinterpretation, harm the patient. By his action, the physician made the malpractice possible, and so should be held to pay damages."

Your attorney might respond, "The patient has a right to choose his own health provider. We cannot pass judgment on that provider. If we had withheld the information he asked for, he would be even more likely to err in the patient's treatment. In this case we're damned if we do and damned if we don't. We made the decision to give out the information rather than be secretive. It is possible the patient would have been harmed whichever we did, and we should not be held responsible."

Is there a way out of this dilemma? Yes; you can go to court *before* making your decision and ask for an advisory opinion. The procedure differs among the fifty states; your attorney will advise you. You may want to tell the patient or the nonmedical practitioner, "Our attorney tells us we should not make the patient's chart available to you without a court order. If you wish to apply for such an order, and obtain one, we'll be glad to comply." Once you have such an order, you are clear of all blame no matter what happens to the patient.

When they do arise, hassles over charts are more likely to be within the professional "family." Just why isn't always clear from court records. But it happened, for example, in a New York case. A patient apparently changed physicians. The new physician asked a hospital to let him take the chart and x-rays for review. The hospital refused. It may have said something like, "This new physician is not a member of our staff, nor does he have privileges here. The chart is our property and too valuable to hand out to anyone who asks; we might never get it back."

The court didn't buy that argument. It split the knot rather neatly by saying in effect, "All right, then, we won't ask the hospital to turn over the chart—but it must make the chart available *on hospital premises* to the new physician. It must do so under proper viewing conditions, and as often, within reason, as the physician needs to see them."

Suppose that your office gets a request from a former patient's attorney to see the patient's chart. Your first thought, naturally enough, is that the attorney is preparing a malpractice suit against you. And your impulse is to declare, "No! No! Never!" Well, now, don't panic. The attorney has a note from the patient authorizing you to turn over the chart. Must you do so? You need not, but it may be wiser to do so.

Here's why: Not every unhappy patient who goes to an attorney has a justifiable claim. (In fact, a large San Francisco law firm that specializes in malpractice cases and has expert medical consultants available, will take *only one case in twenty* that comes in their doors.) The attorney for your patient has heard the patient's story. Now he wants to know yours. He can evaluate the merits by reviewing the chart. He could very well conclude that his client doesn't have a case and drop the matter.

What if you decide to stonewall it and refuse to let the attorney look at the chart? Then she'll probably file suit and get a court order (a subpoena, usually) to produce it. You must obey that order, or you risk jail. So you might as well be gracious about it in the first place and acquiesce. First, however, phone your own attorney and tell him what's going on. He may have some comments based on the law in your particular state and advise about contacting your insurance carrier.

There's another situation where your chart may be subpoenaed. This will depend to a considerable extent on your type of practice. That involves patients who are involved in workers' compensation cases. People who are injured as a result of their employment, or who become ill because of an industrial gas or chemical, have claims against their employers. The employers must carry workers' compensation insurance. So it's the insurance company that pays the lost wages and medical expenses and sometimes the rehabilitation expenses. Where the employer company has more injuries a year than is normal for that type of business, it is likely to experience a raise in insurance rates.

As a result, there will be times when a company will reject a claim, causing the patient-employee to sue the company. Then one side or the other will want to know more about the patient's past medical history. They'll subpoena the chart to see if perhaps the patient had a preexisting lung condition, for example, or a slipped disk, or something else.

In most large cities there are companies that specialize in photocopying charts of hospitals and physicians, and they will do so with very little disturbance to your office procedures. Just be sure you get a copy of the subpoena and fasten it into the chart as a permanent record.

No matter how competent and how careful a physician is, he or she is bound to feel queasy when first faced with a malpractice suit. There's bound to be a feverish review of the chart, an anxious self-questioning: Did I leave something undone that might have contributed to a better result? Did I do something that might be questioned? Was medication right? Surgery unquestioningly indicated?

More than one health professional has panicked and tried to alter the course of history. Perhaps rereading the chart she thinks, "Maybe I should have given this patient a course of penicillin. I don't think it was really needed, but it might look better on the record if a jury has to see it." So she does a little creative restructuring, going back and writing in under various dates the amounts she might have but didn't actually give the patient.

Of course, that's entirely unethical—and no sharp malpractice attorney is going to be fooled. First, on cross examination, he will show the chart to the doctor, ask if it's in her handwriting, or made under her direction, and whether the dates truly reflect the treatment given and the medication administered. The doctor gives the expected affirmative answer.

Later in the trial, the attorney calls a handwriting expert.

ATTORNEY: Mr. Davis, I show you the record prepared by Dr. Blank. Would you say, as an expert, that all the entries you examined were made at or about the dates indicated for them?

MR. DAVIS: No sir.

ATTORNEY: Please point out those that were not made at the times indicated.

MR. DAVIS: There are six items on the record that refer to penicillin treatment that were not made on or about the dates indicated.

ATTORNEY: And what are those six items?

MR. DAVIS: These were items that refer to penicillin administration on June 3, June 7, June 11, June 15, June 20, and June 26.

ATTORNEY: Can you tell us approximately when they *were* made?

MR. DAVIS: Our chemical, spectroscopic, and other tests indicate they were made more recently; probably in February or March of the following year, and apparently all on the same day.

The unfortunate Dr. Blank may have been entirely blameless. Her treatment may have been professionally correct in all respects. But by her foolish act she furnished the rope for her own hanging. For what jury is going to believe *anything* she says now after she has been caught in a lie made under oath?

Dr. Blank's attorney may make strenuous efforts to reha-
bilitate his client by showing that penicillin wasn't really necessary—but that's not likely to overcome the jury's strong
suspicions of Dr. Blank's unworthiness. Of course, altering a
chart is unwise not only for a physician, but also for nurses,
therapists, or others who may make entries.

When you open a chart for Mrs. Jones, you don't anticipate that chart becoming part of a court record. You set it up
in the usual way, make the usual entries, and see that it is
available when needed by the physician and returned to the
medical librarian when it is not. But there might some day be
a need to show that record in court for some legal purpose—
not necessarily a malpractice suit.

To allow you to testify from that chart or even to let it be
looked at by the court, it must meet certain requirements. It
must have been made in the course of professional atten-
dance, and it must be complete, accurate, and timely as well
as being the original. What does the law mean by "timely"? It
means made at the time of the event or as soon thereafter as
practical.

Let's say that the respiration therapist performs a procedure on a patient, and what with the overload and pressure,
doesn't make the entry before he goes on his two-week vacation. But he hadn't forgotten, and as soon as he returns, he
makes an accurate entry showing what was done and all
other necessary information.

Then comes a day when a court decision depends on that
chart. Your side wants to introduce it into evidence. The
attorney calls the therapist.

ATTORNEY:	Mr. Smith, were all of these entries made on the dates indicated, or short-ly thereafter?
MR. SMITH:	All but one, sir. It was made as soon as I got back from vacation two weeks later.
ATTORNEY:	Your honor, we offer this chart as Exhibit 5.
ATTORNEY FOR THE OTHER SIDE:	Objection, your honor! The testimony

shows an item not entered in a timely manner. Therefore, I move that the chart cannot be entered into evidence.

THE COURT: So ordered.

The result is that your important evidence cannot be used. You're safe enough if an entry is made the day following; everyone knows there's never enough time in medical settings. But don't let it go much longer than that. On a Friday night before a three-day holiday, better accrue a little overtime and do it rather than hold it over to the following week.

What do you do when a patient wants to review his or her chart? Until quite recently it was the practice to deny any such review. Now, however, a number of states have enacted patients' rights laws. Under them, the patient need only make a written request to a physician or hospital and pay a photocopying fee to obtain his or her chart.

The laws have been criticized on two grounds. One is that few patients are sufficiently skilled in medical terminology and practice to fully understand the entries. The other is that the physician may sometimes, in his or her professional judgment, feel that a complete revelation of condition may have an adverse effect on the patient, particularly one who is emotionally unstable or in fragile health. In that case, there may be provision in the state law permitting release to a relative or close friend rather than directly to the patient. In such a situation, first talk to your attorney.

What are the rights of employers to see the charts of patients? We've seen that governmental agencies, welfare departments, police, and grand juries can't see them without the consent of the patient. The employer is in a slightly different category. It is one thing to hire a person who is competent for the job; it is another to know something of his health history. Applicants are not always truthful; how is the employer to know if a healthy-looking applicant may not already have asbestosis or AIDS or a chronically bad back? Plainly she won't want to employ someone, spend time and money training him, and then have him "fold" because of physical inability or other medical cause.

If the employer is an airline, railroad company, or nuclear power plant, there is a question of public safety. An alcoholic or substance abuser in a critical occupation may cost the lives of many innocent victims. Shouldn't the employer have the right—perhaps even the duty—to find out the facts about a potential worker? The answer may well be yes, provided that he has the worker's consent. The medical agency can rely on that consent and show the chart. It should be careful, however, to reveal only those portions that relate to employment. Everything else should remain confidential unless the consent refers to "any and all information" in the chart.

The patient hasn't been seen or heard from for fifteen years. Is there any need to keep his chart in the overburdened files? Yes, there is. You may, however, reduce them to microfilm, depending on state law. Again, best check with your attorney. Should the chart be kept filed even though the statute of limitations may be three, four, or five years? Yes, because those statutes don't bar *every* patient from filing suits within that time.

The problem is that such statutes don't start to run until the time of discovery of the malpractice. In one early case, a patient had surgery. Sixteen years went by. Then she had surgery again, for an unrelated ailment. The second surgeon found a surgical sponge the first one had left. The patient promptly sued the estate of the first surgeon (he had meanwhile died), and the executor said, in effect, "Oh, no. You can't claim damages now. The statute of limitations has long since run out." The executor was wrong. The statute ran not from the date of the first surgery but from the date of discovery of the negligence.

Another exception to the statute of limitation is the patient who is a minor. Usually, a minor can sue through a guardian if there are grounds for a law suit. But not necessarily. The law allows minors to wait until they become adults if they wish. So if an infant is injured at birth through the negligence of the obstetrician, he has twenty-one years, plus the state's statute of limitation of one, two or more years, to file. This would be a pretty rare situation, but it has happened and can happen again. So perhaps twenty-three years or so for the retention of files isn't too much in cases like these. That's a long time to keep a bundle of papers—but there may come a time when you'll be glad you did.

QUESTIONS

1. You are office manager for a small medical group. One of the physicians has a patient, George P. Mongo, whom you haven't seen for a long time. One day a woman comes in, identifies herself as a police investigator, and explains: "We are looking for a dangerous criminal named George Mongo. We understand that he was a patient of yours at one time. We have very little information on him, and we're not sure that your George P. Mongo is the George Mongo we're looking for. If I could see your chart for just a few moments, to get his last address, some information such as scars, physical measurements, and so on, it would be most helpful to his capture."

   You happen to know that your Mongo is a very suspicious character and is very likely the man they're after. Should you refuse to give any information whatever about the patient? Or turn the file over? Or say that you must wait for the doctor's approval? Or say that you can't without either the patient's waiver or a court order? Would your answer be different if you knew for sure that your patient is not the man?

2. Your office has seen Mrs. Blank through one pregnancy and one miscarriage, and she appeared satisfied with the results. Now, however, a nurse midwife phones and says that Mrs. Blank is having her, the midwife, for her present pregnancy. (Midwifery is legal in that particular state.) She would like to see Mrs. Blank's chart to assist her in proper care of the patient. Should you provide the chart? May you legally refuse? Must you provide it if the midwife obtains a written request from the patient asking you to turn over the chart?

3. The director of personnel for a large international airline contacts your office. She tells you one of their top pilots appears to act differently than usual. He has taken several days off for a claimed stomachache, and twice he stumbled getting off a plane but was not hurt. She wants to see his chart to determine if he is taking medication, if he has a concealed illness (since he will not be examined by their company doctor), or whether he has shown indications of alcohol or substance abuse. The pilot has also refused to give written consent to

your office for review of his chart. The director says, "I understand you don't normally do this, but this man is at the controls of a 180-passenger aircraft, and we have a tremendous responsibility to the people who fly with him." Should you comply and let the director see the chart? Should you refuse, on grounds of patient confidentiality? Would it be proper for you simply to explain verbally that he has a problem (if you know of one), or has not? Would the law hold you responsible if you *didn't* tell the director that the pilot is under treatment for a serious nerve disorder and the plane crashes as a result?

4. The patient, Mr. Bender, is extremely difficult. H is in late middle age, working to support his widowed, invalid daughter. He is suffering from several chronic conditions, including some that are psychosomatic. His instability has been controlled to a degree with medication. Now, following an examination and tests, you learn that he has inoperable cancer. You enter your findings in his chart but do not tell him, believing, reasonably enough, that revelation may cause a dangerous reaction.

Soon after, you receive a phone call from Mr. Bender's daughter. She says, "Daddy is convinced you aren't telling him everything. He tells me he's going to demand that you show him his chart under the patient's rights law of this state. Do you have any objection to letting him see it?"

You say, cautiously, "Generally speaking, most medical offices feel patients won't know what the medical notes really mean, and some, like your father, are likely to be greatly disturbed. I hope you can persuade him not to ask for his chart." The daughter says, "I'll try, but you know how difficult my father can be once he makes up his mind."

You know—and now must decide your course of action before he appears. Should you tell him that he can't see his chart because of your long-standing office policy? Should you show him the chart and explain the meaning of the entries? Or show it and not explain the entries? Should you tell the daughter his condition and let her break the news? If you firmly believe that the law is bad, are you justified in refusing to follow it? What steps might you take to see if there is a way around this problem within the limits laid down by the state?

3

Who Did That?

Are you responsible for injuring a patient if you have not been adequately trained?

∎

Can you be sued for doing something that is ethically wrong?

∎

Can you be sued if someone under your supervision injures a patient?

∎

If a nurse's aide injures a patient, who else in the "chain" to the top might be liable?

Not long ago, an eminent surgeon hired a highly qualified nurse. The nurse was a young man with impeccable references who adapted quickly and well to the office routine. The office included a surgical suite with several small consultation and examination rooms attached.

Then a woman patient who had come in for facial surgery was found in the office—dead. Examination disclosed that she had received an excessive amount of a sleep-inducing drug. It also disclosed she had been sexually abused while under the influence of the drug. The nurse was arrested and confessed to the crime. Later, authorities learned that he had similarly abused another patient, who fortunately, recovered from the experience.

The dead woman's next of kin, and the living woman, plainly had civil cases for large amounts against the nurse. The nurse, who was later committed to an institution, had no funds. It was, of course, the surgeon who had to settle with the cases and did so through his insurance company. After the settlements were made, the company canceled the surgeon's insurance, which created a severe coverage problem for him.

This is an extreme case, which illustrates how a completely blameless physician can be held responsible for many thousands of dollars in damages for an employee's wrongful acts. The legal basis for this kind of responsibility is well established. It is an ancient rule called *respondeat superior*, which means "the master must pay for the servant's wrongdoing." The theory is that the "master" (today's "employer") has received the benefit of the employee's service and has a duty to see that the employee does no wrong while rendering that service.

You see many examples of this rule in most areas of our society. Let someone drive your car who has an accident— and you (or your insurer) pays the damages. A security guard in a department store shoves a customer, who falls and is injured. The department store as well as the security guard would have to pay. Or a utility company service person damages your stove while fixing the pilot light. The company is responsible for the wrongful act. In the medical field, "top liability" is usually the hospital, nursing home, physician, or the physician's medical corporation.

Within the medical office there are several types of employees who might commit errors or wrong acts for which they personally, and the physicians operating the office, might be responsible. These include R.N.s, medical aides, medical assistants, technicians, and to a lesser degree, those in the "back room" who handle the paperwork, typing, and records.

An example: A medical assistant directs a new aide to prepare a hypodermic. The aide appears to be doing as directed, but through inexperience or carelessness uses the wrong medication and a patient is injured. As employers, the physicians would without question be responsible for damages, and so would the medical assistant who directed the procedure. Why? Because that person delegated a job to an unqualified person. It was his or her duty to supervise the aide to whatever degree required. The medical assistant could not assume that no matter how well-meaning and conscientious, the aide would have the skill required.

Suppose that instead of an unlicensed medical aide, the person who prepared the wrong hypodermic had been an R.N. or licensed practical nurse (L.P.N. or L.V.N.)? Then the courts would very likely hold that the directing medical assistant would be competent to prepare the hypodermic properly. The medical assistant would be "off the hook" but not the physicians or the R.N. or L.P.N.

The safe rule is to delegate properly. The supervisor, or other person giving directions, must know which patient and which service to assign. The person or supervisor or other person giving directions must know which patient and which services may be safely entrusted to others.

Similar incidents can happen in hospitals or other health facilities. For example, an instructor in a teaching hospital is giving assignments to student nurses concerning actual patients. To one she says, "Carla, while I'm working with Linda, will you prepare the preop medication for the patient in Room 4?" Then the instructor busies herself with other students. Carla makes the mistake of assuming that she is to administer the medication as well as prepare it. Although she has had no instruction or experience in giving intramuscular injections, she gives the drug and damages the patient's sciatic nerve.

As we have seen, both the student and instructor, along with the hospital, are liable for the patient's damages. Here the student was in error by not following directions properly. She knew she had not had that particular instruction and so should have questioned her instructor. The instructor was at fault for not communicating clearly in view of the student's inexperience, and for failing to supervise adequately. Had she done so, the incident would not have happened.

CATASTROPHIC ERROR

Not only employing physicians or hospitals, but everyone in the organization, should be aware of the terrible risks that can come from using unqualified people. A Los Angeles case ended not only in a huge demand award, but an anguished family, a destroyed husband and father, and certainly terrible psychological burdens for those responsible. In that case a postop patient who had spinal fusion was put in a private room with oxygen outlets. The regular recovery room was already filled to capacity. Someone assigned a nursing aide to look after the patient. The aide (said to have had only three weeks' experience) was told to call the nurse if she saw any signs of trouble.

Unfortunately, the aide had not been trained in recognizing such signs. When the patient's changing condition required oxygen, the aide did not act. By the time an experienced person came in to check the patient, it was already too late. The patient sustained severe and permanent brain damage, condemning him to a vegetative state for the rest of his life. The judgment against the hospital was about $1.4 million, the second largest award ever given up to that time. The hospital, employer of the unfortunate nursing aide, paid the amount through its insurer.

REAL-WORLD PROBLEMS

Today, there are strong pressures to "thin out" staff as much as possible consistent with good patient care. Often this takes the form of assigning as much routine technical work as possible to the least experienced (and least paid) employees. Nor is it uncommon for experienced people to have more work than can reasonably be accomplished in the time available. These problems come up more frequently in hospitals, clinics, and the larger physicians' offices, but small offices may also be involved.

Suppose that the senior medical assistant in a large physicians' office faces a staff shortage because of jobs not budgeted for. In one facility where this was the case, staff simply could not carry out all orders for patients in the time available. Discussions with the chief administrator did not help. So those members of the staff directly responsible for patient care used the rule that when a nurse or other health professional must deviate from the physician's order, the reason for the deviation must be charted.

They began to write in the charts, for example, "No medication administrated at 5:00 P.M. because of insufficient staff to carry out order." This was enough to prod the administrator into acting. His solution may have helped the staff but not necessarily the patients. The administrative M.D. instructed the physicians to write fewer orders. One hopes that better solutions can be found.

The point here is that health workers should use any legitimate device to get themselves off the legal hook. An overworked staff is more likely to make mistakes—and mistakes can be very, very expensive. A more diplomatic approach would be for staff members in this situation to *document* questionable events. This would mean making notes of names, places, dates, times, witnesses, and what happened, what should have happened, or what didn't happen—all carefully and objectively detailed. If possible, the nurses' appraisals and conclusions should be added. Copies would be circulated through appropriate channels to top administration.

Suppose that there is no satisfactory response to this? Then send another factual, objective communication through channels. This should point out that the conditions described in the original report have not yet been corrected. Add that as a result, danger to patients still exists, with possible danger of malpractice suits. That should work. If it doesn't, continue to keep your copies of communications and take the matter up with administration from time to time. This will be legal proof that (1) staff is doing everything possible to correct the dangerous conditions, and (2) that the administration had ample notice but did not act.

STATE LAWS VARY

The degrees of control over training and supervision vary among the fifty states. Thus there can be problems when an employer, including physicians' offices, hospitals, or other agencies, wants an experienced person to teach medical procedures to unlicensed employees. The person who is asked to do this should carefully check his or her right to do so, if at all, and if so, to what degree. Some medical tasks are clearly forbidden. These may include injections, administration of anesthesia, respiratory therapy, x-ray, and other procedures that call for a high degree of judgment and technical skill.

Economics in recent years have brought about some rules, but not all, by any means. If you have a question and cannot obtain satisfactory information from your supervisor or employer, you may want to consult with one of the associations in your state for the particular health discipline involved. Or you may refer to your state's practice act, which it will have for each licensed health profession. There may also be regulations that spell out just what each one can and cannot do.

WORD FROM THE TOP

The appellate courts of many states have ruled out what is and is not proper care of patients. Most of these cases are malpractice suits, aimed at those most able to pay substantial damages—physicians, hospitals, and other health facilities. Health staff members are often mentioned in the reports. In addition to these appeal courts, whose reports are available, there are many more cases that do not go beyond the trial court level, and are either settled, or in which no one appeals to a higher court.

There seems to be a disposition of the courts to be more concerned with matters of substance than with technical points. For example, in the *Foster Memorial Hospital* case, a young patient had preoperative medication administered by nurses who were not licensed in the state. One was licensed in another state and her papers had not yet been processed for the state where she was employed; the other had been a licensee in Great Britain for many years but was not admitted here.

After carefully examining the record, and hearing testimony, the court said there was no evidence that a nurse licensed in this state would have been more constant and skillful in observing the child for symptoms indicating too much medication. Nor was there evidence that the child displayed symptoms of drug reaction, and only eight minutes elapsed between the time the child was observed to be sleeping quietly with the bed rails up and the time when she fell. The court added that "a hospital is obliged to furnish a patient with the services and care of competent nurses possessing that degree of skill and learning customarily applied in the same community, and such care and diligence must be measured by the capacity of the patient to care for himself, but limited by the rule that no one is required to guard against or take measures to avert that which a reasonable person under the circumstances would not anticipate as likely to happen." These rules also apply to physicians' offices, clinics, nursing homes, and other health facilities; and to health personnel other than nurses who may directly or indirectly furnish services to patients.

In *Valentin v. La Societé Française*, the minor patient was recovering from hernia surgery. He was normal for 8 days, then began showing signs of distress. This turned out to be tetanus. This was diagnosed by the resident, who instructed the supervisor of nurses to call the attending physician. Then he left for the day. One surgeon was on vacation, another had not yet reached the hospital. Over a three day period, the alarmed mother insisted that nurses call any other doctor, and finally one was brought in, who immediately transferred the patient to the county hospital for tetanus injections and treatment. But it was too late—the patient died.

The California appeals court said, "For a supervisory nurse to permit a patient recovering from a major operation to suffer symptoms indicating a growing pathology for three days without medical care merely because the attending physicians were not available is a type of conduct that is negligence." The court mentioned other decisions bearing on care of patients, of interest because of the wide range of situations covered: "It has been held negligence for a surgeon to fail to discover a hemorrhage which he had caused or for him to refuse to suture the operative wound...for nurses to allow a patient to be burned by an electric heating pad...for the management of a hospital to allow the continued use of a lamp after the insulation on its key used for turning on the light had broken off, exposing the metal...for a sanitarium in caring for alcoholics to leave a window unguarded through which a delirious patient might plunge...."

These are only a few of the situations that can occur not only in hospitals but in offices and institutions as well. One need not be an experienced professional to spot dangerous situations; even an inexperienced, new employee might see a frayed electrical cord, for example, that others have overlooked and bring it to the attention of his or her supervisor.

STEPS TO SUPERVISORIAL SUCCESS

You do not need the word "Supervisor" on your nameplate to actually *be* a supervisor. You are one in the eyes of the law if you only review the work occasionally, or help another person perform medically related tasks. These rules can therefore be valuable to you:

1. Delegate only those duties that may legally be delegated.
2. Delegate only to those who are competent to carry out the delegated acts.
3. Instruct and supervise subordinates until you are sure they understand and are able to perform their duties properly.
4. Call the attention of the administration to dangers and document them carefully in writing.

REFERENCES

Butler v. Northwestern Hospital of Minn ., 278 NW 37.

LIPMAN, MICHEL Are You Legally Responsible for What She Did? *RN Magazine*, July 1971.

McDonald v. Foster Memorial . 170 CA2d 85.

Valentin v. La Societé Française, 76 Ca2d 1.

QUESTIONS

1. The supervisor delegates two medical assistants to see that a newly admitted patient is put to bed and given medication for deep depression, as there had been threats of suicide. The assistants take the patient to a fifth-floor room. They check it to make sure that there are no scissors, knives, or anything that might be used harmfully. One assistant goes for bedding, the other for a food tray. They lock the patient in, expecting to be back every few minutes. While they are gone, the patient squirms through a small window, dives out, and ends his life on the pavement below. The patient's family sues the assistants, the physician in charge, and the facility. They claim that there was negligence; that the assistants should have known that a suicidal patient might jump from a window if not watched—and they ask for damages.

   Was the patient's action something the experienced assistants should have foreseen? If so, should a court find them negligent? If the assistants are found negligent, is the physician or the facility responsible for what they did?

   The test of liability here is whether or not an ordinarily prudent person could have foreseen that a suicidal patient may have gone through a window if left unattended. How would you decide this question? Why?

2. You are an experienced and highly qualified registered nurse—and now have become a nurse supervisor. A young physician, only recently in practice, orders a powerful medication for an ailing infant. You are fully familiar with that medication and its use and side effects. You tactfully suggest that he might want to reduce the dosage by about half. He responds, "Don't you think I know what I'm doing?" When you continue to object, he says, "Oh, go ahead and do it, nurse. I'll take full responsibility for the treatment."

Should you do as ordered? Should you tell him that you'll only do it if he writes in the chart that he does take full responsibility? Should you refuse unless he consults with the chief of staff or other senior physician? Should you go over his head to an appropriate hospital official?

4

The Well-Buttoned Lip

Can you be sued for defamation if you tell a co-worker that the new medical transcriber is incompetent and is probably on drugs?

∎

The boss tells you in private that you are a poor worker, a troublemaker, and should never have been hired—all untrue. Can you sue him for defamation?

∎

Is it defamation to tell a friend truthfully that an unmarried patient in your office is pregnant?

∎

You repeat a scandalous bit of gossip you heard and believed was true. Can you as well as the original speaker be sued?

During lunch in the hospital lounge, you whisper to your companion, "There's that repulsive new Dr. Johnson. I hear he's not a Harvard graduate at all and that he's badly botched some of his cases. I can't understand how he ever got a license!" That statement is clearly slanderous and could get you sued, and very likely fired, if Dr. Johnson ever hears about it. As a *practical* matter, he may never hear about it. Your friend may be discreet enough not to mention what you said. So you may get by with it this time. But the medical people in a hospital or office usually form a tight little community and news, gossip, and other information gets around fast. If you have unconfirmed information about someone, keep it to yourself. If it's something that *should* be mentioned to someone, you'll learn later here how to handle it.

THE WHAT AND WHY OF DEFAMATION

Are defamation suits a real hazard to medical assistants? They don't happen every day, nor to many people, but they are a possible risk and important enough for you to know about. And for good reason. A false accusation could get someone fired, ruin a career, result in loss of a professional license. So it's no wonder that a person defamed will react strongly. They sue not only for money but to establish in the eyes of the community that they are really blameless.

What is defamation? The law says that it is scandalous words about someone which tend to injure the person's reputation. If the defamation is *spoken*, it is *slander*. If it is *written*, it is *libel*. Either way, if you maliciously say that someone is a criminal or a crook in his or her business dealings, that is grounds enough for damages. Sometimes special damages may be caused by the false and malicious statements. The statements must in fact be false. Truth is usually a defense. If you say that someone spent time in jail as a wife beater, and the statement is true, that person has no case for defamation.

But truth may not be a defense in every case. In the famed *Melvin v. Reid* case many years ago, a studio made and advertised a silent movie, *The Red Kimono*. It told the story of a woman who had led a very unconventional life and who was tried, but acquitted, in a murder case. The woman, who had since rehabilitated herself and become well known and well liked in her community, sued. The studio pointed out that everything they'd said was true. But the court said that while this was not defamation, it *was* an invasion of the woman's privacy—and awarded her the judgment.

So it's not enough to prove that your statements are true; you must also be sure that they don't invade the person's privacy. Invasion of privacy is closely related to breach of confidentiality, which we discussed in the section "State of the Chart."

THE TRUTH SHALL (SOMETIMES) SET YOU FREE

There are four kinds of statements that can be defamatory:

1. A false statement that hurts someone in his or her job or profession,
2. A false accusation of a serious crime,
3. A false statement that a woman is unchaste,
4. A false statement that someone has a "loathsome dis-ease," generally venereal, but there might be others, such as leprosy.

If defamation is based on *false* statements or accusations, a statement or accusation that is *true* would be a defense, would it not? Generally, yes. Your office manager hires a new file clerk who just happens to be from the same midwestern town from which you came. You don't know her, but she knows who you are. And she whispers around the office that you were once convicted of homicide. She says that you were sentenced to a term in jail.

The senior partner in your office hears the rumor and asks you privately to tell her about it. You explain that a crisis in your former marriage caused you sudden great anguish. You took a couple of drinks, then attempted to drive your car home. The night was stormy and the drinks affected your judgment. You hit and killed a pedestrian. You were charged with manslaughter and convicted. But because of the extenuating circumstances, the judge suspended your sentence. Your insurance company paid the victim a substantial settlement.

The senior partner doesn't believe that you should lose your job, which you have done well. But you feel badly used and believe that the new girl acted maliciously in spreading the report. You sue her for slander. Your attorney tells the court that this was a malicious statement and that it implied you had committed a far more serious crime.

Here the court would very likely rule that, first, in slander it doesn't matter if the person was malicious or not*; and further, that the hurtful statement was in fact true. Manslaughter *is* homicide even though completely unintentional; and you *were* sentenced even though the sentence was suspended. So you would lose the case.

Here, truth is a complete defense. Does that mean that every falsity is a slander? No, it doesn't. Perhaps you remember the kindergarten rejoinder to some contentious playmate: "Sticks and stones may break my bones, but names will never hurt me!" This is a good attitude but one that we unfortunately lose sight of when we mature. Names *do* hurt us: sometimes very severely, as where someone loses a job because of rumors, or patients leave, or credit is impaired, as someone sues over a false report in a credit record about a bankruptcy filing.

A practitioner, whom we'll call Dr. Jackson, was very skilled in his specialty and very proud of the fact. He seems to have been an arrogant and difficult person to be around for anything but treatment. Someone whose feelings he'd hurt told friends that "Dr. Jackson is nothing but a criminal. He's an Eichman, a Hitler, even!" Dr. Jackson heard it, and was not amused. He filed suit against the speaker, claiming that this characterization hurt him in his profession and that it was false.

The court said it didn't matter if it were false or not;

---

*The question of malice comes up in defamation by publications. An Israeli official sued *Time* magazine for saying that he was involved in a massacre of Palestinians. The statement was false. But the court said that it must be malicious as well. So the official lost.

these words, ugly as they might be, say nothing about the quality of his patient care or professional qualifications. They reflect only on his character, and since he hasn't proved damages for injury to his character, he must lose the law suit.

There was a similar result in a case where a professional person was called "flamboyant." The court said that only meant that he had a showy manner, and that's not necessarily bad. So he too failed in his suit.

GOOD NAME RATHER THAN GREAT RICHES

On the other hand, a hospital worker said that one of the doctors was drunk the previous Wednesday and unable to give full medical service and attention to an injured patient. The doctor sued. The speaker said in defense that lots of people drank too much at times, and he hadn't implied that the doctor lacked professional skill. Did that comment reflect on the doctor's professional abilities? The court said that it did. If the average person heard that a certain physician was drunk when a patient needed attention, that person would certainly not want to become his patient. And the doctor won his case.

The question of truth as a defense in slander is not as easy as it sounds. A claim examiner said that Dr. Smith's medical report and traction treatment didn't impress him, and that it "was the consensus of opinion that Dr. Smith often overtreated his patients."

The defendant's counsel said that, first, it was entirely true that the medical report and treatment didn't impress him, and second, that the opinions of others were matters of fact—a truthful, if unflattering set of beliefs by others was also the truth, and therefore not slanderous. The appeal court in South Carolina said that this made no difference; that the claim examiner's statements were slanderous in themselves because they reflected on the physician's professional integrity.

This opinion seems open to question. Is the court saying that it's all right for people to speak well of a professional person but all wrong to say anything against him or her? And what is a reputation but a comingling of peoples' reactions to a person? We'll see later that it is not always slander to speak badly of someone under some circumstances.

THE MOVING FINGER WRITES

Slander is a close relative of libel. Slander is based on hurtful *spoken* words. Libel is concerned with *written* words. *Defamation* means either libel or slander.

If a newspaper columnist writes falsely that a respiration therapist (whom he identifies) badly injured a patient during intubation because the therapist was on drugs, that is libel. But suppose that the columnist appears on a local radio show and makes the same remark verbally? Is that slander or libel? The law makes a somewhat arbitrary distinction: If the statement is spontaneous—"ad-libbed"—it is considered spoken. However, if it is read from a written script, that is said to be libel. In either case, it is defamation.

For the health worker, libel might be important in the case of reports written to the personnel file, or a written response by a former employer. Suppose that you lose your job as a medical clerk and apply to a different health facility for employment. The personnel director seems impressed and promises to give careful consideration to hiring you. You leave with a good feeling. A few days later you're told, "Sorry, we find you don't meet our qualifications."

That's quite a jolt. But you have a friend working at that facility who tells you the truth. The director checked back with your former employer. That employer wrote, "John's work with us was adequate. However, on his shift we noted a loss of hospital supplies, including drugs, to which he had access. For that reason we would not rehire him if we had a job opening of this kind."

You're furious, because you never once took unauthorized supplies. So you sue for damages. You point out that the letter in effect calls you a thief. And you show that you were refused employment at least once because of that unjustified statement. Do you win damages? No.

jolt [´dʒoult] – толчок, бешенка
shift – смена,

THE POINT OF PRIVILEGE

Why no damages, when the health facility told an untruth about you that caused you to lose out on a job? Because there's an *exception* to the general rule, called *privilege.* Privileged communications are defined as "those which cannot be made the ground of an action for defamation." In John's case, the court held that the facility had a duty to relate the facts, as it knew them, in the interest of society. There was no malice here; the facility responded to a reference request with the facts *as it understood them.* And it stated those supposed facts to another facility that had a legitimate interest in knowing them.

It was certainly important for your prospective employer to know what kind of person you are. Suppose that you really had taken those supplies? Suppose you really did use or sell the drugs that were missing? There'd be a good chance that you'd do the same to your new employer. That would not only cause financial loss but might result in harm to a patient—such as switching medications.

This puts the medical worker in a difficult position. You have certain ethical duties in a medical setting that you would not have, for example, in a warehouse or department store. You might discover that a fellow employee is pocketing and carrying out small items that he or she has stolen from stock. This might disturb you, but you do not have a duty to report it if you do not wish to. You may well reason that (1) the loss is only financial, (2) the employer probably has security people whose specific job is to catch thieves, and (3) the job you were hired for doesn't require you to blow whistles.

It's different in medical offices and hospitals. You're dealing with lives, not pocketbooks. Patients may die as a result of inferior treatment, inattention, wrong treatment, wrong medication, or other preventable behavior. No matter what your job is, you may know something that someone has done, or is doing, that could have harmful results.

Suppose that a staff member or a physician is treating a patient in a harmful way—through negligence, ignorance, malice, or incompetency. May you give this information to someone with authority to do something about it? *Should* you give it? If you do, are you protected by the rule of *privilege?* To *whom* do you report it? Certainly not the patient's relatives, who are concerned about his or her recovery, or anyone not involved in the case. But there may be a time and place for you to speak your mind. First, be reasonably sure of your facts. You may have seen a wrongful act. Or there may be documentation that shows it. Or you know that other people around you—workers or patients—support the complaint.

The code of ethics of one major professional group says that the person should act "to safeguard the patient when his care and safety are affected by incompetent, unethical, or illegal conduct of any person." How does a medical employee "act to safeguard?" By following the chain of command in making the report. Tell your supervisor, stating just the facts as you know them: what you saw, when you saw it, what you heard, who said it, who else was present, what the effect appeared to be.

Assume that you believe in good faith that a physician did not respond quickly enough when told that a post-op patient was bleeding heavily. You could report this to your supervisor and your report would be considered privileged—even though it turned out that you were mistaken. You could not be sued for slander.

What should your supervisor do? The supervisor should see that your observation is sent through channels to whoever has the ultimate responsibility for that physician's actions. This might be chief of the department, the administrator, or in an office setting, perhaps one of the senior members of the firm.

You might find yourself in a situation where you're in a small office, and perhaps the physician is the only one. Then you might be justified in reporting to your state physician licensing bureau or quality control board. What you say would be privileged and you could not be held responsible for slander even if you were wrong.

TELLING IT TO THE JUDGE

What you say in court may also be privileged—provided that you answer just the questions asked you—not more, not less.

Here's an example of "overanswering": The attorney asks, "Now are you saying with absolute certainty that on January 17, you saw this person take a quantity of Demoral without authority?" And the witness replies, "No, but she stole drugs on other dates." That witness could be in trouble. He was asked about one specific event. Everything else is irrelevant. And it might not be protected by privilege, so the witness could be sued in another action.

This rule applies no matter in what kind of court or hearing you might appear, where you are sworn to tell the truth. That would include licensing boards, quality control boards, grand jury appearances, and so on. Conceivably, you might be asked to tell your story before a peer review committee. This would be a group of physicians, generally in a hospital setting, considering actions by a particular health professional. You would not be sworn, because peer groups do not have legal authority. However, what you say in response to their questions would be privileged and you would be protected against a possible slander action.

STRENGTHENING YOUR CASE

There are steps that you can take if you see inappropriate action taking place around you and want to avoid a possible defamation suit if you report it. The first is to document what you see and hear. Keep your own confidential notebook. Most situations such as those of theft of drugs, negligent behavior, drinking, and so on, take place over a period of time. Make your notes brief. For example: June 8, 19,...at 10 P.M. Mr. Smith reported to the lab 1/2 hour late. He appeared to walk unsteadily and asked me if Ms. Jones, the lab supervisor, was on the floor. I told him she was always off on Tuesdays, and this was Tuesday. A little later he again asked me where Mrs. Jones was. His speech was slurred and I smelled alcohol about him. Ms. Peterson was also in the lab when he asked me the second time.

June 10, evening shift, 11:15 P.M. I entered the lab with a specimen. Mr. Smith was there alone, in the act of drinking from a bottle with a whiskey label. He laughed when he saw me and said, "Wanna drink, kid?" I said no, that drinking on the job was forbidden and could get him fired. He said, "Fire me? Best lab man they ever had? Forget it." I left.

If you are a physician or supervisor, and responsible for employees, you will certainly want to document any behavior by someone you feel you may have to terminate. This is an appropriate part of your job, and it might be well to let your superior know you are doing so. If you are not in a supervising capacity, you can still keep your own unofficial notes. Of course, you won't discuss them with anyone.

The next step to safeguard against a suit is to check your malpractice policy, or get one if that is possible. Check to see if defamation, libel, or slander are covered. If your policy doesn't cover this, you should contact your insurance broker and ask to have a rider attached to your policy. The cost is usually very small.

The third deterrent to a defamation suit against you is the expense. Legal talent comes high these days. The person suing may have to make a substantial payment in advance, and possibly put up a bond. Also, if he or she loses the case, there will be your costs to be paid. And if the defamation is really only technical, without real damage, the award could be very small.

This last is not complete protection. If the person claiming defamation is a professional, he or she will be very conscious of losing a valuable license. To protect that license, they may be willing to spend a substantial amount for lawyers, court fees, reporter fees, bond, jury fees, and so on. So if you must speak ill of someone, do so only to those who need to know for public protection, speak only the truth, and be alert to the fact that words can indeed hurt. They can hurt not only those they're aimed at, but also the one who aims them. So when you must speak, do so wisely and courageously and you will be safe from legal retaliation.

REFERENCES

Jordan v. Lewis, 247 NYS.2d 650.

DENNISTON, LYLE, Supreme Court Strikes Off in New Direction, *California Lawyer*, Vol. 6, No. 1, January 1986.

Woodward v. So. Carolina Farm Bureau, SC, 282 SE2 599.

McBride v. Merrill Dow, 1983, 230 App. DC 403, 717 F.2d 1460.

QUESTIONS

1. A patient walks angrily out of a physician's office and up to where you are working. She says, "I don't believe that doctor knows a thing about my condition! I think he's a quack!" Are all the elements of slander here? Discuss.

2. The chief resident calls you into his private office, closes the door, and says, "I don't care to have anyone else hear this. I want to tell you I am very dissatisfied with your work. You are lazy, you have no interest in the work, and you are not competent to work in a medical office." Has he committed slander? Why? Why not?

3. A patient comes in suffering from an apparent psychosomatic condition. You diagnose this as the result of some recent major emotional event. When you suggest this to the patient, he says, "You're absolutely right. Three months ago I killed my wife and sent her in a trunk to Knoxville, Tennessee." A few days later a police detective calls and wants to know what you treated him for and what was said. You realize the importance of the questions, but you also have in mind medical tenets (and the law in many states) that a patient's disclosures, if related to his treatment, are confidential unless he waives the protection. How should you respond?

5

Keeping Your License

If you have never committed a wrongful act, can a
licensing board take away your license to practice?

■

May you have an attorney with you during an
appearance before a licensing board?

■

Can a licensee be disciplined for using profane language in front of a patient?

■

At what point may a licensee's employer bring
charges for unprofessional conduct?

Anyone who has a license to practice as a professional has had to work hard to obtain it. Among those who must have a license before working at their chosen callings are physicians, lawyers, high-level accountants, real estate brokers and agents, dentists, registered nurses, licensed vocational (or practical) nurses, pharmacists, hair dressers and barbers, and certain therapists, along with private detectives, collection agents, and court reporters.

The reasoning behind licensing is simple: To prevent abuses, lawmakers wanted to set up safeguards so that only qualified people might engage in those activities. Also, by setting up licensing boards, they have a "handle" on those who obtained licenses and later prove unworthy of them. The purpose is to protect patients, clients, and customers from people who may harm them, fail to give appropriate service, or swindle them.

Loss of a license can very often mean loss of a livelihood, and those who have them cherish them. They will not part with them willingly. Lawyers may fight disbarment for several years; physicians are equally tenacious. Often such fights have been indirect. The person charged may not have a good defense for what he or she did but will challenge the board's power to act. In effect, they say, "Regardless of what I may have done, this board doesn't have the right to act against me in this case."

WAS THE HEARING FAIR?

How much power do these state boards have? Should they be allowed to function in the place of the courts where questions of a person's license are so important?

Ms. Peck, as we'll call her, was a licensed nurse who had been with the clinic for many years. She was one of the best around, and she knew it. She also had her own medical theories, and some of them weren't in accordance with accepted allotropic standards. She also had strong opinions about physicians. She'd often say to the younger nurses, "Physicians? I've seen 'em come and seen 'em go, and there isn't one of them couldn't profit by a big dose of common sense."

Nor did she hesitate to give her own medical views to the staff physicians. "Doctor, if I may make a suggestion..."—and most of them, recognizing her long experience, listened. But one day Ms. Peck went too far. A young woman patient was being treated for an obscure condition of the lower bowel. A battery of tests showed inconclusive results. Ms. Peck found the patient sitting alone in an office, crying. She said, "I'm so discouraged. I've been coming here for months, and nothing they do seems to do me any good."

Ms. Peck said, "Not surprising. Some of these wonder-boys look so hard for flyspecks that they can't see the elephant standing there. Your trouble is that your intestinal flora have been killed off by all this medication you've been taking. You need those bacilli in your digestive processes. Now here's what you do. First, throw out all your medications. Next, go on a vegetarian diet. Then, get yourself some acidophilus at a health food store, and take it every day for ten days. I guarantee you'll feel better!"

That was the moment she heard a voice behind her. She whirled around to see the flushed face of the patient's doctor. "It's quite possible, Ms. Peck, that I might not see an elephant. But I'm not so blind I can't see a flagrant violation of professional ethics under my nose! Believe me, madam, you'll be hearing more about this!" And he walked out.

A week later, Ms. Peck received an order from the state board of registered nurses. She was to show cause why her license should not be revoked. The order said she was charged with making a medical diagnosis and communicating that diagnosis to a patient. She was also charged with prescribing treatment. Both acts were permissible only to licensed physicians and surgeons.

The letter enclosed informed her that she might have an attorney present at the hearing and that she or her attorney would have the right to cross-examine witnesses against her. She could also present witnesses or evidence in her defense.

The hearing took place in an administrative courtroom. A quorum of the state board of registered nurses was present. The board's attorney called the patient for whom Ms. Peck had diagnosed.

The attorney said, "Mrs. Bellman, did Ms. Peck tell you what your medical difficulty was?"

The witness said, "She told me what she thought was wrong with me, yes."

"And did she tell you what treatment to take for it?"

"Yes."

"Which was?"

"To throw out my medications, go on a vegetarian diet, and take acidophilus."

"Thank you, Mrs. Bellman, that is all. Cross-examine."

Ms. Peck's attorney asked, "Mrs. Bellman, did you follow Ms. Peck's advice?"

"Yes, I did."

"With what results?"

"After three weeks, my problem disappeared completely."

"I see. And did Ms. Peck ask, or did you ever pay her anything for her services?"

"No; nothing."

"That is all, Mrs. Bellman. Thank you."

The board's attorney then called Mrs. Bellman's doctor and had the doctor repeat the conversation he had heard between Ms. Peck and Mrs. Bellman.

He asked, "And you recognized that what Ms. Peck had told this patient was a serious violation of medical ethics as well as of the law?"

"I did."

"That's all, doctor. Thank you."

Ms. Peck's lawyer cross examined. "Doctor, you were treating Mrs. Bellman for almost a year before this incident, were you not.?

"Yes."

"What were you treating her *for*?"

"Well, we tried a number of treatments—"

"You misunderstand, doctor; what specific dysfunction did she have? An ulcer, diverticulosis, what?"

"Our tests were not conclusive. I couldn't say positively. There was an intestinal problem for which we could not determine the underlying cause."

"Have you any way of explaining why you could not

relieve Mrs. Bellman during a year of intensive tests when Ms. Peck's suggestion apparently did so in three weeks?"

"Objection!" The board's attorney was on his feet.

Ms. Peck's attorney said, "I withdraw the question," and smiled at the witness. He called as a witness the administrator of the clinic where Ms. Peck worked.

The administrator testified, "She is an excellent nurse; a little ascerbic at times, but very knowledgeable and very good with the patients."

Fair Hearing Tested

A few days later the board ruled. It said that Ms. Peck had been guilty of unprofessional conduct. They ordered her license suspended for one year, with thirty days active. What that meant in practice, was that the nurse could not work for a month but was in effect on probation for the remaining 11 months of the year.

Ms. Peck had her lawyer appeal to a judicial court. He said, "The suspension or revocation of the license of a professional person is too serious a matter to be left to the discretion of nonjudicial persons. The people on the board are respected figures in medicine, nursing, and the allied healing arts. But they are not trained in the law. They were unable to give her the fair and impartial hearing guaranteed by the Constitution. Their decision should be reversed."

The appeal court didn't see it that way. The judges pointed out that the law in that state specifically said that only licensed physicians and surgeons might communicate their diagnosis to a patient, or prescribe medical treatment. It didn't take a lawyer to understand that Ms. Peck violated that law. Moreover, a reading of the record showed that she had received a fair and impartial hearing. She had been allowed to testify and to produce witnesses, she was allowed to have her attorney with her, and she was allowed to present evidence. There was no indication of bias or prejudice on the part of those who judged her. Therefore, the board's decision was affirmed, and Ms. Peck had to accept the suspension ordered.

BOARD POWERS ARE BROAD

The power of disciplinary boards usually extends beyond questions dealing with patients in a professional capacity. A man we shall call Evar Sorensen, working as a licensed respiratory technician, became acquainted with a young woman patient. Sarah had been a drug addict and was on probation for a narcotics charge at the time. Apparently, their friendship became close, for Evar removed a supply of drugs from the hospital stock and removed it to his apartment. When Sarah was discharged from the hospital, she moved in with Evar. A few weeks later, officers arrested Sarah at the apartment and seized a quantity of the drugs. Evar admitted taking them from the hospital.

Evar's state disciplinary board held a hearing to revoke his respiratory technician's license. They based this on his criminal behavior. Evar's attorney objected strenuously to introduction of evidence about the drugs being in his home. The attorney said, "The arrest had to do with Sarah. Evar was not suspected of anything at the time. Therefore, the search of his apartment was illegal and all evidence having to do with drugs must be suppressed."

The board ordered revocation of Evar's license. Evar appealed. The appeal court denied his appeal, thus upholding the board's ruling.

Some boards have the power to issue a preliminary or interim revocation immediately on receiving evidence that the licensee has been convicted of a crime involving moral turpitude. The licensee has the right to appear and show, for example, that the conviction was of someone else of the same name, or that the crime did not involve moral turpitude or perhaps temporary insanity. The board may then rescind its order.

WHAT A BOARD CAN DO

To lose a professional license does not necessarily mean that it is lost for all time. While powers and functions differ widely, in general, disciplinary boards may:

- Dismiss the charges

- Admonish the licensee only
- Suspend the license for a limited time
- Revoke the license
- Take other appropriate action

Revocation of license is the most serious penalty. But even revocation is not necessary forever. At some future time—two years, three, five—he or she may petition for reinstatement. If conditions have changed, if the person has become rehabilitated, the board may review the case and set aside its previous order, restoring the license.

A license revocation does not necessarily bar the person from all medically related jobs. One might teach, if qualified, or work as a computer operator, secretary, steward, statistician, or other position that does not require a license.

DRUGS LOOM LARGE

The types of cases coming before boards vary throughout the United States. As our first illustration indicates, you don't have to be guilty of breaking a *law* to have been guilty of unprofessional conduct. To avoid an unintentional violation, read and know the code of ethics for your own professional group as well as the law (usually a particular state code section) that relates to your group. It's also a good idea to be familiar with state law relating to *physicians'* rights and duty. Ms. Peck, in our first example, might not have found a prohibition against revealing diagnosis to a patient—but it would certainly be in the written law for doctors.

Among the most common complaints reaching the boards are, as you might expect, those involving drugs. Despite controls, temptation is sometimes overpowering, and a worker who has access to them may yield. One, for example, falsified a patient's control cards on the night shift. He would note that the drug had been administered—but actually kept it for himself. He was charged by the police for "buying, receiving, and concealing stolen property, and possession of narcotics." In addition to criminal charges, he lost his license. A licensee might be disciplined for deceit in obtaining a license—or for incompetence, gross negligence, immorality, or involvement in criminal activities.

NOT A ONE-WAY STREET

Don't panic if a charge is made against you. You have rights, including the right to proper notice, to a fair hearing, and to rights similar to those you would have in court, except for having a jury: Members of disciplinary boards usually sit as both judge and jury. This isn't quite the same as being in court, where you might have a separate jury. But those decisions are always subject to review by an appeal court.

Geraldine, for example, was brought before her state board charged with unprofessional conduct, gross incompetence, and "habits rendering the licensee unsafe to take care of the sick." Well, it appears that what she did was let a woman patient sit in the hospital waiting room for an hour before the obstetrician arrived. When he did arrive, as he later claimed, she "insulted the patient, using profane language that caused her mental anguish and emotional disturbance."

What had she said? She had said, "Well, the goddamned fool. If she hasn't sense enough to tell us that she is going to have a baby, let her have the baby right here in the lobby!" The board was horrified. It found Geraldine guilty and ordered a penalty. Geraldine appealed.

The state supreme court reversed the board's decision, saying that the board had "failed to specify the ground for 'habits rendering a licensee unsafe to care for the sick,'" and adding, "If it were to be found that profanity is a ground for revoking a license, there could be a serious depletion in the ranks of all the professions!"

SAFEGUARDING YOUR LICENSE

In "Ethics for the CPA," members of that profession are told it is not enough to avoid improprieties; they must also avoid the *appearance* of impropriety. Obviously, a dictum like this is open to broad interpretation. But it does make a point; you are judged by more than your impeccable behavior at your place of work. This may be unfair. You may well argue that your lifestyle is your own business. Which it is. But people—including patients—are not always tolerant or broadminded. Many perceive a professional person as someone in whon they place their trust—if not their lives—and they want to feel that person is somewhat superior. So the wise course is not only to shun evil but to avoid even its appearance.

What if, despite your best efforts, you think you are in danger of being fired? If its a matter of a general staff cutback for reasons of economy, you have no remedy but to find a new job. But if you think your supervisors feel that you are incompetent, careless, come in late too often or not at all, or may be sampling the Demerol, there are protective measures you can take.

First, be aware that employers are no longer free to fire anyone for any reason at any time—especially not if you've been employed a considerable time. You can sometimes sue and win a substantial judgment for wrongful discharge, especially where the employer has failed to document your misdeeds. In court, your attorney will ask, "You say that this person was late reporting for her shift on many occasions. What were the dates? How late was she? How much time does this add up to in a month? Was that time made up? Was her salary charged with the lost time? If the supervisor hasn't kept documentation, the facility is in deep trouble. Your attorney will also ask, "Was this person counseled regarding her tardiness? Was she warned that she might be subject to discipline? If you discussed it with her, could not adjustments have been made to allow for transportation or other problems?"

Second, if you suspect trouble, consult your attorney. Ask if it would be appropriate for you to request the facility to let you see your personnel record and what, if any, derogatory information it might contain. Be guided by his or her advice.

Also, keep what you know to yourself. Don't talk to anyone about your fears or your plans. Meanwhile, keep notes, including time, place, and names and addresses of people likely to be involved. Note where the documents or files are located and who has possession of them. If worse comes to worst, your attorney can subpoena them in your suit or in your defense.

The disciplinary power of the state disciplinary boards is not intended to threaten you as a competent professional person. Rather, they are intended to protect you and your professional colleagues against those who willfully or through incompetence harm professionals and their patients.

QUESTIONS

1. Dr. X has a large practice, mainly of Hollywood and New York celebrities. An investigation by the state medical licensing board discloses an unusually large number of prescriptions that he wrote for a wide variety of narcotics. The board wants to revoke or suspend Dr. X's license. He responds that he committed no violations; that celebrity patients as a group are prone to anxiety attacks and other ailments requiring medication such as he prescribed; and that in any event a physician has full discretion in selecting appropriate treatment for his patients. What should the ruling be in this case? Suppose that several patients had died from overdosing. Would that affect your answer?

2. In the four years since she obtained her registered nurse license, Zelda has been an outstanding practitioner, cheerful, patient, reliable, well liked. Then it is discovered that she lied on her license application. She said "no" to a question asking if she had been convicted of a felony in the five preceding years. In fact, she had been, and was put on probation. Action was brought to revoke her license. Her attorney argued that licensing was designed to protect patients and that Zelda had acted in exemplary fashion to protect patients ever since she became a nurse. The attorney said there was absolutely no indication that Zelda's past misdeed could cause her to harm patients in any way. What do you think of the argument? Is a major falsehood on her application a bar to her continuing in her profession?

6

Professional Liability: Mephistopheles Rides Again

Can a medical assistant be sued for malpractice?

∎

Just what is professional liability?

∎

Need you be a medical professional to be sued for malpractice?

∎

Do you need malpractice insurance if your employer is covered?

∎

Where do you go to get malpractice insurance?

∎

What can you do if such insurance is not available to you?

The term *professional liability* is really a euphemism for *malpractice*. Neither is popular in the lexicography of the medical world. Small wonder; the insurance premiums of physicians and hospitals have become astronomical. If you're mad at your physician, just say, "I hear they're raising malpractice insurance rates again!" Then watch him turn white, clutch at his chest, or both.

The reason for the huge premiums is not primarily the greed of insurance companies. In fact, they haven't been particularly eager to enter the field at all. The exposure—or risk—of suits is very high, and judgments can carry seven-figure price tags. On a nationwide basis, the combined risk is in the billions of dollars—and this risk must be spread over a relatively small "population." Every claim, from a few hundred dollars for a broken tooth, to a million plus for great disability or death, must be paid in the long run by the profession itself—then passed along to patients in the form of higher fees and charges.

Some states have tinkered with legislation to control or "cap" malpractice awards. These efforts have not yet had conclusive results. Mainly, the newer laws have been compromises between two major interest groups. One group consists of the insurance companies representing physicians, hospitals, and indirectly, the public. They tell legislators that malpractice awards are out of bounds, and will continue to grow, with the effect of raising health care costs. They want to see a cap on awards and a limit on the time within which patients may file suits. They say that health professionals are now forced to practice "defensive medicine," requiring batteries of expensive tests and procedures which they would not normally consider necessary.

The other group is made up of trial lawyers, who also serve the public, especially those people who have been or will some day be injured or killed by substandard treatment. What cap, or price, they ask, can you put on damages to a 28-year-old man, supporting a wife and children, who is made a vegetable by negligent medical care? He will need continuing care for possibly 50 years, his family will need support, his children must be educated. Meantime, living costs will increase. How can you cap that kind of disaster? Further, say the lawyers, most malpractice specialists are very selective about the cases for which they sue: possibly fewer than 10 percent. They say they can't *afford* to take questionable cases because they often must make enormous investments of investigative and research time before going to trial. And if they lose, they may be out of pocket for as much as $200,000.

The problem is, there is merit on both sides. The public wants a zero-defects health establishment. No mistakes. No errors. No goofs. Yet that establishment is made up of human beings: men and women who are, for the most part, dedicated, conscientious, highly skilled people. They may have problems, too. They may have bad days because of personal problems. Some may use controlled substances illicitly or overuse alcohol. Or, in a busy, understaffed, overworked establishment, there may be an honest mistake, a mistaken order, a critical timed medication overlooked. Considering the heavy load and the enormous responsibility of the medical organization, it is remarkable that relatively few harmful incidents occur.

LIABILITY OF MEDICAL ASSISTANTS

When block busting malpractice suits are filed, they will almost invariably target the physician or the hospital, or both. The reason is simple: Physicians and hospitals have the money, or their insurance companies do. The individual medical employee who may actually have done the negligent act is usually not wealthy, or even affluent. However, the one who employs that person is also responsible.

Not every mistake or error is malpractice. Whatever the physician or medical assistant does should be within the standard of care for his or her particular level of expertise. The standard of care has been defined in this way: A physician is under no legal duty to treat anyone (with certain exceptions). However, once he or she does undertake to treat a patient and enters into a physician/patient relationship, he or she has a duty to conform to the "standard of care" *by which he or she is to exercise that degree of knowledge, skill, and care which a similarly trained physician would ordinarily exercise in a similar case, under like circumstances, in the same or similar locality.* If there is failure to follow that standard, the physician may be considered negligent, and if a patient is injured as a result, he or she may be liable in damages. The law does not require the highest professional skill, only reasonable and ordinary skill and care.

A physician is not liable for malpractice every time a treatment or diagnosis has an unfortunate result. It is only if someone is injured because he "failed to possess and use that degree of learning, skill, and care in diagnosing and treating...that a reasonably competent physician would employ in the same circumstances." In effect, did he make a mistake that most other doctors with his qualifications would not have made?

Every health care provider is subject to a similar rule. This applies to registered nurses, licensed vocational nurses, medical technicians, therapists, psychiatrists, psychologists, nurses' aides, pharmacists, chiropractors, podiatrists, medical assistants, and others engaged in the care of patients. We've seen how this operates in the section "Who Did That?"

So let's say *you* are working in a medical center. Patients in your department come and go continually for treatment, or walk-away surgery. One patient goes in for surgery, leaving her clothing and purse in an area over which you have supervision. She returns in two or three hours and finds that her purse is missing.

It was, she claims, full of money and jewelry—and can prove it. All right, you were there. You were responsible. Where's the purse? You don't know? Then you and the center will be asked to pay. The center refuses. The patient sues.

This situation can have one of two possible results for you:

- The center has an insurance policy that covers it and all employees for all acts of employees in the course of their duties by any person making a claim for any cause arising out of that employment.

or

- The center has an insurance policy that covers it but does not cover employees.

If your employer is in the second group, you are in an unenviable position. You're going to have to hire an experienced attorney to represent you—an expense. And you are going to have to take time off from work for depositions, possibly hearings, and certainly a trial if the case is not settled. More expense—very likely, more than you can conveniently afford.

Most employers *do* cover their employees for negligent acts against patients. But that's no sure panacea. There are different kinds of insurance. If you ask your supervisor if the employer has malpractice coverage, the answer will probably be, "Of course we have insurance. We couldn't operate without it." But that doesn't really answer your question. What you *really* need to know is whether you *personally* are covered. The sad fact is that some of the top management people don't know themselves. They've probably never read the policy, and if they had, they may not have understood the jaw-breaking legal language.

In an actual case, a new employee asked the administrator if he, the employee, was covered. The administrator said yes, he was, and that it wasn't necessary for him to carry his own insurance. The employee believed the administrator—and, of course, it wasn't long before a patient sued that establishment for malpractice. The employee was named in the suit. And guess what—he wasn't covered at all!

The administrator simply hadn't known what she was talking about. Most likely she'd heard that from someone else, who'd heard it from someone else, who was wrong to start with. So the employee had to retain his own attorneys, and if he lost, pay damages out of his own pocket.

FIND OUT FOR SURE

There is one sure way to find out what the medical employer's professional liability (malpractice) insurance policy covers. That is to request a "certificate of insurance," issued by the insurance company. You can request this yourself, or your professional organization may be able to do this for you. You might want to have your attorney review the certificate for you, and explain what it means and whether there are any "holes" in it.

The obvious first thing is whether you, as a professional medical assistant, are covered for negligent acts that cause injury to a patient. You also want to know just *when* the policy covers you, and *what it covers*. You'll probably find that you have coverage only for the hours actually worked on the job. Protection? Certainly—but not total, absolute, sure-fire all-around protection! Suppose that someone you supervise does a wrongful act when you are properly absent?

That's not a far-out supposition. In a case actually submitted to an insurance company, the employee went out to lunch. While she was gone, her new assistant tried to help a patient change garments. There was a slip and fall, and the supervising employee was sued. Did the medical center's insurance cover her? No! Because the employee wasn't at work for the center at the time; she was at lunch on her own time. The policy covered only when she was actually employed *and on the job!* Fortunately, this assistant had been wise enough to buy her own, round-the-clock malpractice insurance, and *that* covered her.

Another point to watch for is *property damage*. Are you covered if you accidentally break or lose something belonging to a patient? One frequent source of claims in hospitals—and sometimes in offices—is the breaking of a patient's dentures. The patient will wrap them in tissues, and the employee looking after the patient may not notice them in among the other soiled tissues, pick them up, and—*clang*—there's a lot of expensive porcelain all over the floor.

Sometimes you can face some really weird situations. Here's another insurance file case. Miss Aames (as we'll call her) was a medical assistant in a large medical office. There had been some unexplained shortages in the Demerol supply. One evening Miss Aames noticed Mr. Miller (also fictitiously named) with his back to her at the drug chest. She said nothing then, but when she saw him acting suspiciously around the drug chest a second time, she notified her employers. When the administrator and a detective approached Mr. Miller to question him, he popped something into his mouth and swallowed it. They arrested Miller and charged him with theft of an uncontrolled substance.

The judge thought the evidence was too weak. He dismissed the case. Miller promptly sued the medical office, the physicians, the administrator, and Miss Aames for false arrest. Did the medical office's malpractice insurance cover Miss Aames? It did not! *Why* not? Because the false arrest wasn't malpractice. It wasn't something that grew out of professional conduct. Neither is assault and battery, unlawful restraint, or a number of other acts unrelated to your professional activities.

Your employer may be very thoughtful and considerate of employees and very desirous of good relations. But when it comes to considerable sums of money, they have their partners, stockholders, and others to answer to. So when you are out on a limb, they may regretfully, but efficiently, try to saw you off.

Case in point: A hospital was about to discharge an elderly patient who was a very, *very* important person. The gentleman had made substantial contributions to the hospital and there was every expectation of more to come. Not surprisingly, he had superlative attention from every employee in the place. When this VIP was ready to leave, the discharge nurse said to the medical assistant, "Miss Drake, please wheel Mr. Bemis as far as our front door. Mr. Bemis's chauffeur will come up and help him down the stairs into his limousine."

"Sure, Mrs. Martin," the young lady said, "Glad to help."

But when Miss Drake got to the front door, she saw through the door that the limousine was just driving in. So she helped Mr. Bemis through the door, across the portico, and was starting with him down the stairs as the chauffeur came to a stop. At that moment, Mr. Bemis stumbled, and the medical assistant was unable to hold him. Down he tumbled—and sustained a painful and long-to-heal broken hip. After his second medical discharge, Mr. Bemis sued the hospital for a large sum and named Miss Drake in the legal papers.

The hospital's attorneys said, "We aren't responsible for this regretable accident. You see, Miss Drake failed to follow her instructions. She was only to take Mr. Bemis to the door. Instead, she went through the door and started down the steps with him. By that act she left our employment and in effect was off on a frolic of her own. She and she alone is responsible."

The poignant moral is that no matter how benign and kindly an employing organization may be, in the malpractice jungle, it's everyone for himself or herself!

BLUE SKY LIGHTNING

One thing you must keep in mind about malpractice suits: *You can be sued even when you're clearly in the right*. And even the most inconsequential suits may cost you time and money. Edna Parsons, for example, was carrying an armload of medical records. As she passed through a ward, an elderly patient who had been hospitalized for stroke got on her feet, apparently to go to bathroom facilities. As Ms. Parsons came near, the patient stumbled and grabbed for her. Surprised, Ms. Parsons dropped her files. Thrown off balance, she stumbled away so that the patient was left without support. The patient swayed, lost her balance, and fell, breaking a hip. She filed suit.

The case never went to trial. It seems very doubtful, on this set of facts, that the patient had a valid claim. Ms. Parsons can hardly be said to have been negligent; she herself might have been injured by the patient's loss of balance. Nevertheless, her insurance company paid the patient a fairly substantial settlement amount to receive a release of claim.

STATUTES OF LIMITATION

A statute of limitation is a state law that says how long a person has within which to file a suit. If he or she files *after* the time limit, the court will throw out the case. The length of time varies from state to state; usually, it's a year or two from the time the malpractice takes place. When this time expires, lawyers speak of it as "the statute of limitations has run." Most of us use a less cumbersome phrase: we say that the claim has "outlawed."

Even though in your particular job you never take a

patient's temperature or feel a pulse, the statute of limitations is important to you. Assume you are only involved with records. In the event of a malpractice suit, the lawyers for the injured person (the plaintiff) will examine those records under subpoena or court order. They and their medical experts will go over them with a very finetooth comb. They want to know exactly what was done, when, and whether this was consistent with good medical practice.

No physician, no nurse, no technician can remember every detail of a case that surfaces months or years later. Even if they could, they could be torn to pieces by cross examination without records to support them. That is why every record, chart, report, or memorandum must be *complete, legible,* and *accurate.* But you may ask, you only have to keep these records for the time of the statute of limitations, isn't that true? Because the patient can't sue then?

No, it's not true. First, you need good records in case the patient has a recurrence of his or her problem many years later. The physician has to know what he did then so that he can properly diagnose and treat now. Most hospitals and medical offices do keep records for many years—and then microfilm them. Where some or all of the patients' records are computerized, the storage problem is less acute. However, before destroying any paper records, the office or hospital should check with their attorney.

What most medical people don't know is that the statute of limitations *doesn't necessarily start running at the time of the treatment.* It would be very unfair if it did. Older cases have noted that sponges were floating around inside a patient for three, five, or more years. The case of Dr. Mengel arose some time ago and is instructive here. The doctor, located in Pennsylvania, did some abdominal surgery on a woman. Apparently she continued to experience discomfort for a long time, because sixteen years later she had more abdominal surgery, by another surgeon. Dr. Mengel had died in the interim. The second surgeon found a surgical sponge supposedly left in her by his predecessor. The patient sued Dr. Mengel's estate.

Attorneys for the estate said, "Oh, no, no. We have a two-year statute here and you come in sixteen years later and expect to enforce your claim?" Despite the lapse of time, the court ruled against the estate and in favor of the patient. The court said that while the injury began at the time of the surgery, the statute only began to run at the time of the *discovery* of the injury.

There's another situation where the statute is stopped. That is where the injury is to a *minor*. Of course, minors can and almost always do sue for injuries through a *guardian ad litem*—an adult whom the court will accept as someone standing in the place of the minor for the purposes of the suit. But the minor need not sue through a guardian during his minority. He may wait until he becomes a legal adult and then sue. Theoretically, at least, an obstetrician, and possibly his assistants, can be sued twenty-one years and nine months, plus the state limitation period, after the claimed injury!

The advent of superdrugs in recent years opens another can of worms. Powerful drugs may have sinister side effects, some of them surfacing many years afterward, but unknown at the time of treatment. It seems reasonable to suppose that such claims will not be barred by state statutes of limitations.

GOOD SAMARITAN LAWS

Good Samaritan laws are state laws which say in effect that if, as a health care professional, you give care to an accident victim, you are exempt from a later claim of malpractice. The idea is to encourage physicians and others with health care training to help in emergency situations. By doing so in good faith, without gross negligence, they are protected. Beyond that basic idea, the various state laws are very different.

Nowhere (except in Vermont) are you *required* to help someone in an emergency situation—such as an auto accident, a cardiac arrest, or unconsciousness. Everywhere else, if you do elect to help the person, you need only to do so to the extent of your skill and training, and with consideration of the circumstances, such as severe storm conditions, explosion damage, remoteness, and so on.

Although you are not under a legal obligation to help such a victim, you may have an ethical obligation to do so.

The Principles of Medical Ethics of the AMA says that physicians should respond to any requests for help in an emergency. In any event, if you undertake to help at all, you should only treat within the scope of your training and give care appropriate to the situation.

The problem is, what do you do if you're a respiratory technician and the injured person has a broken leg? Probably all you can do is make him as comfortable as possible and keep him warm to avoid shock; then summon paramedics or ambulance to the scene.

If you've had CPR training, take annual review training to keep your skill intact. Recently, a well-meaning person administered CPR to an unconscious man. The person got breathing started, but only after several minutes had passed. During that brief time, the man suffered acute, irreversible brain damage. A grieving relative observed, "It would have been better for everyone if he had been allowed to die."

Whether or not you choose to act is entirely within your own discretion. If you don't, that is your right. If you do, and the victim is injured further, you are probably protected under your state Good Samaritan law. Because of differences, you will be wise to check the wording and see what is or is not required of you. Regardless of wording, it does not appear from legal research that anyone has ever won a lawsuit against a Good Samaritan. Hence the danger of a malpractice charge against you in a situation of this kind is exceedingly remote.

THE INSURANCE MUDDLE

Earlier in this chapter the perils of "going bare" (health care term for going without malpractice insurance) were mentioned. It was pointed out that while *most* hospitals, clinics, medical offices, and other health care centers will cover employees as well as themselves, some may not. And even when there is coverage, the facility or insurance carrier may try to escape liability through a legal loophole. You would be prudent, therefore, to look into carrying your own professional liability insurance. Where can you get this coverage at a reasonable cost?

You're in luck if your professional association offers group malpractice insurance. Associations that have had this service in the past were able to obtain very favorable premium rates. Sign up at once! Your second choice is to see an insurance broker. If you already have auto or home insurance with one, see that broker. The fact that you are already a customer will stimulate him or her to do an appropriate search; brokers don't like to lose good customers and should be able to find a company that will issue you a malpractice policy.

The third possibility is to work out a cooperative arrangement with other employees and your employer to provide a "rider" to the employer's existing malpractice policy so that you are fully covered. You may want to enlist the assistance of an attorney to review the coverage offered you.

A fourth possibility is this: There are group legal services in some areas. It's something like group medical practice. You join the group, paying a monthly or quarterly fee. This entitles you to a range of consultations and services, some probably without further charge, some at a reduced rate. Pick an attorney who is experienced in insurance cases, tell him or her what you do, and ask what the attorney thinks you should do for protection in the absence of available malpractice insurance. Have an understanding that at the first indication of a malpractice problem, you will contact the attorney with full information and that the person will represent you at agreed-upon charges.

GENERAL MALPRACTICE AVOIDANCES

There is little question that some awards to patients for malpractice are entirely justified. When they are it seems nothing short of stupid that the parties cannot negotiate an appropriate settlement. Generally, a hard-fought battle over how much to pay involves a trial, possibly appeals, possibly retrials, which can be more costly than a settlement would be in the first place.

One fairly recent effort to avoid lawsuits is through arbitration. Some health organizations require in their contracts with members that in the event of injury claim, they will arbitrate and try to work out differences with a panel or an arbitrator. Although it is too soon to draw hard-and-fast decisions, it does appear that arbitration is a feasible alternative.

The following suggestions for avoiding malpractice suits will not apply to every reader, because of varying skills, training, occupation, and responsibilities. But almost everyone can benefit by the suggestions designed to make patients feel comfortable with the health care professionals who work with them. Even when the medical results are disappointing, those patients will feel that the physician, nurses, other staff people, and the hospital did everything possible and will not be inclined to start unjustified lawsuits. But where the patient feels slighted, discriminated against, or treated in an offhand or casual manner, he or she may build resentment that explodes into action when the patient's recovery is not up to their expectations.

The medical assistant's role in inducing a comfortable frame of mind is extremely important. It can mean the difference between a satisfied, loyal patient, and one who is angry, resentful and grudge-bearing. Coincident with this frame-of-mind approach, office and hospital staffs can take care that the physical environment will not injure the patient and that all equipment is in good working order and hazard-free.

1. Know what conduct is unlawful, and avoid any such conduct. Take steps necessary to prevent fellow employees or colleagues from such acts.
2. See that the area for which you are responsible is safe and free of hazards. See that equipment is always ready for use.
3. On a regular basis, check insulation on wires for wear, examination tables for possible breakage, instruments for possible defects.
4. Keep your paperwork current and accurate; see that all diagnostic tests have been read and initialed by the physician before filing.
5. See that all patients are treated with equal courtesy and dignity.

6. Make sure that patients' telephone calls are returned as soon as possible.

7. Twenty minutes should be the maximum wait for patients with appointments. If further delay is necessary, explain to the patient; offer coffee or tea, if possible, and a cookie to a child. Report back to the patient frequently.

8. Remember that everything connected with patient care is confidential and not for discussion outside the office.

9. Be sure that signed consent forms have been obtained for procedures.

10. Follow up on missed or canceled appointments.

11. With new patients, make sure that probable costs and payment plans are discussed and agreed on.

12. Professional excellence demands continual education; don't "rest on your oars." In some states, continuing education is mandatory for some professionals.

13. When special instructions must be given to a patient, put them in writing and keep a copy.

14. Take time to listen to patients; some cannot express themselves well. Try to understand the underlying causes of their concerns.

15. When you discharge a patient or withdraw from a case, be sure to document your action fully.

16. Comply fully with the Controlled Substances Act. Document as required.

17. Do not attempt services beyond your scope of training or experience; call in appropriate assistance.

18. Establish careful and thorough policies for the emergency room so that patients' needs are quickly met regardless of circumstances.

19. Where the patient load is large, use a computer to accumulate and analyze patient injury information; take corrective action when trends are discerned.

20. Make periodic inspections of all facilities and equipment.

21. Provide ongoing educational and training programs for all staff as well as for patients.

These suggestions are by no means all-inclusive. No matter what your job is in the medical/health area, you may find some ways to improve your own efficiency and accuracy, and to note and correct any possibility of injury or offense to patients. Yours is not an easy job—but you will find satisfaction in knowing that what you do contributes in some measure to the health and well-being of many people.

QUESTIONS

1. Lydia, a medical technologist, had been with a large medical center for nine years. She was greatly stressed because of a bitter divorce. She cried a lot, slept little. Her job was to examine biopsed tissue under the microscope. One day she reported a specimen as negative. It was in fact positive, and the patient's cancer spread. The patient sued Lydia and the center for malpractice. He said that had she not been negligent, he might have been spared a lot of pain, suffering, and mental anguish. Lydia's attorney told the court, "Not every mistake is necessarily malpractice. Lydia has a legal duty to work within the general standard of knowledge, care, and skill of medical technologists. But that doesn't mean she must be totally accurate in every one of the several thousand examinations she makes each year. There is no proof here that despite this one error, she has failed to meet the established standards of her profession."

   Should Lydia (and the center) have to pay damages? Should the center have had a second technologist to check the findings of the first one? Is there a limit—because of skyrocketing costs—to how much checking and cross-checking medical professionals may be required to do? If Lydia alone was guilty of malpractice, can the center be held as well?

2. A middle-aged man brings his stepson to a private hospital's emergency room. There'd been a fall from a motorcycle. The boy says that he's dizzy; the stepfather explains that the boy has vomited several times. The admissions clerk asks, "How do you intend to pay for the services?" The stepfather replies that they are on welfare; the boy has Medicare. But he doesn't have the card with him. The admissions clerk says, "I can't have the doctor examine him until you have proof that there'll be payment. If you go get the card and bring it back here, I'll see

what I can do." The stepfather and boy leave. But before they get back with the card, the boy is dead.

The general rule of law is that a physician is not duty bound to take every patient. He or she may decline for any of several valid reasons. But should a hospital be bound by the same rule? Is the danger of nonpayment for expensive services a valid reason to refuse aid to an emergency patient? Can the admissions clerk avoid liability by pointing out that she was only *told* about symptoms and saw nothing to indicate an acute emergency? If the court finds the clerk negligent, can the hospital be made to pay the damages? Will the hospital's insurance cover this situation? Will the insurance cover the clerk as well as the hospital—if it does at all?

3. When you are hired by a medical office to supervise the record room, you ask about insurance. "We carry insurance on all employees," you're told. "If you, or any of us who work here, are involved in a medical suit of some kind, the insurance covers you."

So you go to work on a schedule of 36 hours a week. You find that the files are in poor shape, and soon you are staying much longer hours realphabetizing, and sometimes find papers that are misfiled. Then it turns out that the medication ordered for P. J. Johanson really should have been administered to P. I. Johanson. It was in a file that you hadn't gotten to yet. So the wrong person was medicated and suffered severe side effects, because no one noticed the difference in names. There's a lawsuit and you are named one of the defendants. You're served with papers.

You ask what to do and you're told, "Well, we're sorry about this, but there's nothing we can do for you. You see, when you undertook to revise the files, you did it on your own time. So you weren't an employee. So you aren't covered. And I hate to tell you this, but if it's found that you were negligent because you were not an employee for that particular func-tion, we're claiming we're off the hook and that you are totally responsible!"

Which means that you'll have to hire your own attorney—for a minimum of $100 an hour. Now, can you demand and get your legal fees and costs back from the firm you worked for? If you're found blameless, can you get them from the people who sued you?

7

Patients Also Have Legal Problems

What should you do when a stranger comes into the office, hands you a paper labeled "subpoena," and says that he wants to see the medical file on a patient?

∎

In what kinds of situations might your office records be needed with regard to a patient's legal problems?

∎

When should you volunteer information in the hearing of a lawsuit?

∎

What kinds of medical facilities are most likely to be involved in someone else's lawsuit?

There are times when a medical office, hospital, industrial injury clinic, emergency room, or other health facility can be involved in lawsuits that are not directed at or by them. That is when they have information important to a patient's case. The frequency of such involvements depends on the facility's type of practice.

If your facility handles a heavy industrial accident case load, you can expect frequent calls to physicians to testify for or against a worker who has been injured or made ill through his or her employment. In a busy office of this kind, one or more staff members may spend most of their time receiving requests for opinions, docketing deposition and court appearances, filing legal documents, transcribing physician's notes concerning the medical condition of the patient-client, and other law-related tasks.

Usually, this information is required for workers' insurance hearings. The hearings are to decide if the worker actually sustained her health problem as a result of working where she did. If so, how much permanent or temporary disability did she suffer and for how long? Is the patient's illness or injury such that rehabilitative services are needed?

In a typical case, a worker might be sent up a ladder to fix an awning; the ladder was not properly tied down, the worker falls and wrenches her back. She is off work for two weeks before being certified able to return to her job. Normally, the employer's insurance company will pay the worker for her lost time—usually somewhat less than her actual salary, and pay for all related medical and hospital expenses. Most of the time, there are no hearings.

However, the claim may be complicated, or questionable. For example, a 55-year-old shipyard worker may be found to have previously unsuspected asbestosis. It may be that during his working life, he was employed by a series of industries, in some of which he may have been exposed to asbestos. The worker's condition may be severe, and the claim could run into tens or hundreds of thousands of dollars. There's a hearing before a commissioner of the state industrial accident commission; later a civil law suit is filed in court.

Here your office may need to provide evidence as to the patient's condition when first seen, the present condition, and the probable future course of the disease. He may be asked about first exposure, which could be as much as 30 years before the disease shows itself.

SHADOWS CAST BEFORE

In real life the "big scene" of court appearance does not come about with the suddenness of a Perry Mason drama or most television court productions. There's a lot of preparation and paperwork first, some of which will involve the medical facility. There will very likely be telephone calls, correspondence, and possibly informal conferences between attorneys and physicians who are on the same side.

The other side may come into the picture with a subpoena to produce medical files. It may come as a shock to you, because you know that such files are confidential. However, a subpoena is a court order to which you are compelled to respond. Failure could result in possible arrest and imprisonment for contempt of court.

The person presenting the subpoena may be an attorney's employee or from a firm specializing in serving subpoenas and photocopying office records relating to the case. This has the advantage of giving the information required without giving up possession of your original records and file. What should you do when someone presents you with such a subpoena? A good idea is to check the document, note what records are required, and make sure that the subpoena is dated and has a judge or commissioner's name written, typed, or stamped at the bottom. If not, call this to the attention of the physician when you check with him or her before turning over the records. The physician may want to check with the attorney who retained him before taking further steps.

QUESTIONS BEFORE QUESTIONS

So we see that the *subpoena* is the process used to get papers to the other side for use in court. There are three basic kinds of subpoenas. First is the subpoena *duces tecum,* the kind

Patients Also Have Legal Problems

duces tecum — for documents
2
— not for trial / you have
3 — for trial / to
go

we've just discussed, which is used to obtain documents and records. The purpose of a second type of subpoena to take deposition sets a time and place for questioning witnesses under oath *before* a court hearing. The deposition is usually taken in a lawyer's office, before a notary public, while a stenographer takes down the sworn testimony. Either or both sides may ask questions at the deposition.

This proceeding is helpful in "nailing down" the testimony the physicians and other witnesses are likely to give in court. It may also be used to smoke out questionable testimony.

"Now, doctor, you have stated here in court that exposure to asbestosis may not result in disease for twenty years; is that correct?"

"Yes, that's right; about twenty years."

"Doctor, in your deposition of April 8, did you not say, right here on page 19, that the period may be as long as *thirty* years?"

Important point? Yes because it may have been that when the patient worked for the particular company sued, it was twenty-five years ago. One answer would absolve the company; the other would make it liable.

The third type is the subpoena that simply requires you to appear in court and states the time and date. Do not confuse *subpoena* with *summons*. The summons (with an accompanying "complaint" or "declaration") is the first paper filed in a lawsuit. You would not get a summons unless you are being named as one of the defendants. If one or more of the physicians you are associated with is sued for malpractice (or even for a "fender bender" small claims case), she or they would first receive a summons.

THE FACTS OF EVIDENCE

You may, from time to time, have to obtain or take possession of evidence. You may even help create it—as where you take laboratory samples, type or word-process reports, or record a patient's vital signs. Much evidence is in documentary form, but you may also handle physical evidence. Look, for example, at a bullet extracted from a holdup victim. A surgeon removes it, initials it, and places it in a sealed envelope which he dates and signs and which you may sign, too, so that you can identify it later if needed. You put the envelope in a locked compartment until called for. You would probably be asked to testify that you saw the bullet placed in the envelope, saw it sealed, signed the envelope, and kept the envelope in your possession from that time until its delivery to the officers. (Locking the envelope in a compartment to which only you have the key is considered to be in your possession.)

Testimony you give in court is evidence, too. The attorney questions you: "You've testified that you were present in the office when Mrs. Blank came in. I note that the medical record says she was treated 'for hematomas and contusions on face and head.' Would you describe her condition a little more fully?"

"Well, yes; besides the bruises and puffy condition of one eye, she was crying hard. Her hair was in disarray, and she was wearing only a coat over her nightgown, and bedroom slippers."

Notice that this reply is highly factual; there is no subjective opinion that could be objected to by opposing counsel. If you are to testify in any major hearing or trial, the attorney working with the patient or your employers will almost certainly want to meet with you to discuss your testimony. He or she may make suggestions about conservative dress and hairdo and will carefully instruct you just to answer the questions completely, no more and no less. To do otherwise can sometimes have dire results.

WITNESS TO WHAT?

There are a number of other situations where you might be called on to testify. If you are in charge of the medical office's or the health facility's books and records, you might have to appear in court for several reasons. Most common might well be collection cases. A patient who can afford to pay his or her bill hasn't done so. There is no response to your statements. With approval, you assign the account to a collection agency that files suit. If the patient contests the claim, there may be a trial. You would appear with the patient's account sheet (the *original,* not a copy). The attorney representing your side would ask you something like this:

"What is your occupation, Ms. Jones?"

"I am office manager for doctors Littlejohn and Williams."

"Do you have charge of the books and records of the doctors that are kept by them in the course of their professional works?"

"Yes, I do."

"Do you, or does someone under your supervision and direction, enter the charges and payments made by their patients?"

"Yes, I do."

"Will you please refer to the record of the defendant in this case, Charles Gaffney, and tell us if this record of charges and payments show a balance still due the doctors, and if so, what that balance is?"

"Yes, the balance is $1198."

"Which is still unpaid?"

"Yes; still unpaid."

"Thank you, Ms. Jones; I have no further questions at this time."

You may or may not be cross-examined following this testimony. Cross-examination may go in many directions. The defending lawyers might question you concerning dates of visits or treatments (hoping to find that the suit is barred by the lapse of time, a rule that varies from state to state); or there might be questions as to possible wrong entries; or there might be an incorrect balance, with the defendant bringing in canceled checks that he claims were in payment; or there might be some other bookkeeping problem. It is not likely that you'd ever be asked specifics of the medical treatment itself.

A word about small claims courts. These are courts where the money amounts are relatively small—from a few hundred dollars to perhaps $3000, depending on the state. Lawyers may not appear in small claims courts. The people who sue or are sued must represent themselves. They can bring witnesses, however. If your employer is a professional corporation, most small claims courts will require that it can only be represented by a corporate officer—which might be

deed — 내 governmens, act

one of the physicians or an administrator who is an officer such as a vice-president, secretary, or treasurer.

Another possibility is that you might be called as a witness in a disciplinary case brought against a licensed health worker. There the problem might be the person's behavior on the job, questionable handling of drugs, incompetency, or other unprofessional conduct.

In a hospital or nursing home setting, you might be asked to witness a patient's will or other document, such as a deed. Later, you may have to appear in court to confirm that action. Usually, this is a routine matter, taking only a few minutes before a judge or commissioner. But occasionally, the medical worker may have to testify as to the competency of the patient at the time of signing.

Unless you work in nursing or technology, such as an x-ray technician, therapist, medical assistant, or someone working directly with patients, it's not likely that you'll be called as a witness in a malpractice case. Actually, few health people other than the physicians will have much to do with court appearances. But it can happen—and if you should be involved, your testimony could very well be vital to your organization.

HOW TO BE A GOOD WITNESS

Rightly or wrongly, people, jurors, and even judges and lawyers tend to evaluate you by your appearance, manners, and the way you communicate. A shuffling, mumbling old man may be wholly truthful, but he is less likely to be believed, for example, than a well-dressed, unruffled person who answers questions clearly and candidly.

So Rule One is to dress conservatively; a business suit for men, and generally, a tailored suit for women as well. (You may hate this part—stay away from slacks, even if part of a suit. We still have some old-fashioned judges on the bench who have been known to send witnesses home to dress more properly.) If in doubt about what to wear, check with the attorney for your side.

Rule Two: Stay low-key and natural. Don't let opposing counsel make you angry or get you rattled. Stay calm. If you don't understand a question, say "I'm sorry, I don't understand your question." If you don't know the answer, say "I don't know" or "I'm not sure."

The attorney on your side may say, "Now, Mr. Smith, please tell the court what you saw and heard in Ward C on April 10th of this year, in your own words."

Now, you've already talked to the attorney about your testimony, so he knows what you're going to say. But the judge and jury do not. So go ahead, explain the whole thing. Stay with facts only. It's all right to say "The patient was dressed and walking up and down the room. He was red in the face and waving his arms around. He kept shouting for the nurse." Those are all facts. It's not all right to say that he was angry and excited and wanted nursing service. Those would be your opinions, and that's not what is called for. There's a difference between saying that the patient shouted for the nurse and saying that he wanted nursing service. You don't really know that he wanted nursing service; he may have been disoriented and not have known what he wanted. That's the difference, and that's why you must only give facts.

Rule Three, and perhaps the most important: Don't over-answer. Break that rule and you can give away the farm. For example, a physician denies under oath that he had signed a contract for some expensive medical equipment. When shown the contract, he said that it was not his signature. His lawyer put the physician's wife on the stand to confirm that it was not his signature.

The opposing lawyer said, "Mrs. Mason, you are sure this is not your husband's signature?" The lady said, "Oh, absolutely sure. He wasn't even in the room with me and the salesman. He was busy and went out and said to me as he left that I could sign it for him." And that was the ballgame, because by that remark he made his wife his agent for signing the contract and was therefore bound by its terms.

Rule Four: Don't resort to a tranquilizer or a little shot of Smirnoff to steady yourself. Sure, you're going to be a little nervous about going on the stand. But don't worry; you'll do better than you think. You've got the lawyer to guide you, and the judge will help if the other side gets out of line.

Rule Five: Don't memorize your testimony. If you've given a deposition, ask the lawyer (if he or she doesn't ask you) to read it through shortly before the trial. If you have notes, take them along. If there is complicated material, you will generally be allowed to refer to them to refresh your memory.

Rule Six: Watch your attitude. The court is a serious, dignified place, and rightly so; it reflects our desire for a forum where we can expect justice. So be respectful. Don't answer flippantly or try to joke or "ham it up." You'll be running at a high adrenalin level; don't let it make you lose your temper or become belligerent or evasive. A calm, even-tempered, deliberate witness will do the most for his or her side.

If you work in a large urban center, the chances of your somehow being involved in a legal proceeding is considerably greater than if you're located in a small town in the midwest. Should you find yourself headed for court some day, think of it as a wonderful opportunity to see our democracy in action. Courts have been evolving for thousands of years. They're still far from perfect. But they have been responsible for many of the rights and privileges we enjoy today—and in the great majority of instances are composed of men and women striving faithfully and honestly to arrive at fair and just decisions.

QUESTIONS

1. You are the supervisor of vocational nurses in a medical center. One evening, the center is extremely busy; there has been a bus accident and a lot of injured patients are being treated with a very limited staff. There's a big load on one of the newest doctors. He's very busy with a badly injured patient and calls to one of your vocational nurses, "Ms. Fairless, I need a hand here right away."

   The nurse replies, "In just a moment, doctor. I have to enter a medication order in the nursing notes."

   "Never mind that; I've got to have help this moment."

   "But doctor...!"

   "I know, I know. I'll take the responsibility. You get over here *now!*"

   The nurse did as she was told. In the confusion, someone else saw the notes, observed no entry for the urgent medication, and remedicated the patient. There was a reaction; the patient almost died, and later sued the center and the physician.

You're called to trial as a witness and asked, "Ms. Carter, I show you the original nursing notes for the night in question. Do you see an entry here made by Ms. Fairless?"

What should your reply be? Should you say, "No, but there was good reason...." Or, "I'm sure that Ms. Fairless fully intended to make the entry later." Or simply "No," without further explanation?

2. A man half-carries a pale, weeping inarticulate woman into your medical offices. "Hurt her back bad," he mumbles. "Take care of her. I'll be right back; got to park my car."

Examination shows a knife blade driven into the patient's back, with the handle snapped off. You see that the blade is removed, wound appropriately treated and bandaged, and the woman sedated and put to bed. She refuses to say what happened. You call the police to report an apparent assault. The man who brought her in never shows again.

As nurse in charge, you assisted at the woman's treatment. You put the knife blade into a plastic bag and label it. You mark the label "blade removed from Jane Doe's back, January 16, after she was brought in by her intended killer and abandoned." You sign; the treating physician signs. Because you have no safe in the office, you lock it in the drug cabinet, to which only you and the physician have keys.

What steps were taken correctly? Which, if any, were inadvisable?

8

Abused Children and the Health Unit

You suspect that a child being seen at your office or hospital has been abused. What should you do? What should you not do?

∎

Under what circumstances can the child's story be believed?

∎

How believable are the parent's explanations of the child's injuries?

∎

Why are sexual abuse cases harder to prove than physical abuse cases?

∎

What is the position of the health professional who suspects the situation if the child dies as a result of abuse?

There is an estimate that 1 million small children are being abused in the United States today. No one knows if this represents an increase over the past years or, less likely, a decrease. That is because until fairly recently no one realized that there was such a problem. It surfaced in 1962, when C. H. Kempe published his study, *The Battered Child Syndrome.* He and his co-authors described this as children showing evidence of injury or neglect: bone fractures, subdural hematoma, multiple soft-tissue injuries, poor skin hygiene, or malnutrition; or, they said, where the parents' explanations and the clinical findings are inconsistent.

The Kempe study was a beneficial bombshell. Within four years, every one of the states passed laws requiring physicians and other health professionals to report any child injuries that appeared to be the result of abuse. While the fifty states' laws differ, most include particular professionals and nonprofessionals. The list is fairly broad; it includes dentists, residents, interns, religious practitioners, teachers, licensed day care workers and social workers, podiatrists and marriage counselors, child counselors, school superintendents and principals, administrators of public or private summer day camps or child care centers, psychotherapists, and registered nurses.

THE ETHICAL PROBLEM

All child abuse laws, different as they may be, create a difficult ethical problem for health professionals. They are trained to treat the patient's revelations as confidential. There is the very plausible reason that some people in need of medical care will avoid it if what they reveal is not kept secret. Few people getting an abortion, or getting treatment for a social disease, want it known outside medical walls.

Let's assume that a mother bringing in a battered child is questioned by the physician. She responds, "Okay, yes, I'm to blame. I'm very nervous. And the kid whines and cries and makes a big fuss, and I tell him to shut up, and he doesn't, and before I know it, I've grabbed anything around and whacked him with it." How does the physician comply with the reporting law, and remain at peace with his or her ethical obligation not to reveal a patient's secrets?

*заставляющий,
принуждающий, обязывающий*

The problem is difficult. On the one hand, there is said to be a compelling state interest in reporting on abused children. On the other hand, treatment—especially psychotherapy or psychoanalysis—often requires extremely intimate and possibly shocking revelations by patients. If this treatment is not absolutely confidential, the patient will be mistrustful and treatment impossible.

There are some legal indications of relaxation of the strict confidentiality rule: It has been said that no privilege exists when a psychotherapist reasonably believes that a patient is dangerous to himself or others. The disclosure then is weighted in favor of compelling state interest. At least one state, California, gives immunity to psychotherapists from either criminal or civil liability for breach of confidence. That law also takes away the professional's discretion—he or she *must* report child abuse.

*revelation –
открытие, обнаружение, откровение*

PHYSICIANS' LIABILITY

Physicians other than those in psychotherapy must also contend with the reporting laws. One of the earliest damages cases involved a 5-month-old infant, Tommy Robinson. He was admitted to a hospital with a skull fracture. He was treated and returned to his mother a few days later. During the next month, the mother brought him in several times with a series of injuries, including whip welts, puncture wounds, and burned fingertips. The last time, the infant had strangulation marks and had stopped breathing. There was permanent damage. Police arrested the 17-year-old mother's man friend, who was convicted of child beating and jailed.

Tommy's natural father brought a multimillion-dollar suit against four physicians at the hospital who did not report the child's condition. The insurance company compromised the case and a $600,000 trust fund was established for the child's care and treatment.

A later case, *Landeros v. Flood*, went to a state supreme court, which held that the "battered child syndrome" was an established medical diagnosis. The court said that the physician should not have released a child back to the parents after treating injuries that appeared intentionally inflicted. He should have reported the matter, and should have known that after returning the child, it would surely suffer additional physical violence.

OTHER PROFESSIONALS LIABLE

While most of the reported cases involve physicians, there is little doubt that other health professionals may be responsible for failing to report. It depends on whether there is a "reasonably close causal connection between the breaching conduct and the resulting injury...." That is, there must be some duty to the child, express or implied. Without this special relationship, there will not be responsibility.

This was made plain in the case of Joshua DeShaney, who fell into a coma when he was 4 years old. It was the climax of a story well known to the county social services department. Joshua's father Randy was 21 when the child was born in 1979. A year later the parents divorced. The court granted custody of the 1-year-old boy to his father. The father, his girlfriend, and the boy moved to Wisconsin.

In January 1982, the county social services department learned that Randy had been beating and maltreating his son. That appears to have been when Randy's second wife notified police that the child was being abused. The police notified the social service department. Their staff interviewed Randy. "Me? Hit Josh? Naw, not ever." The interviewers did not speak with Joshua. Case closed.

A year later, Joshua turned up in the emergency room and again the social service department was told that there was possible child abuse. They assigned a caseworker to see if there was enough evidence to make Joshua a ward of the juvenile court. The caseworker reported that the suspicion was unfounded. The hospital returned the child to his father, but the department did arrange counseling services for the DeShaneys. The caseworker met several times with the family. She did not always see Joshua, who was beginning to turn up at the hospital with a series of injuries. These included head bumps, a scratched cornea, what the caseworker said

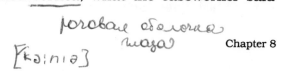

"appeared to look like a cigarette burn," a bloody nose, a boxed ear, and bruised shoulders. Randy said Joshua had hit his head on the toilet.

The caseworker visited the DeShaneys in January 1984 but was told the boy was sleeping. Although it was midday, she did not ask to see him. Randy told her that Joshua had fainted several days before for no reason that he could see.

Suspicion Confirmed

Later, the caseworker told Joshua's mother, Melody DeShaney, that "I just knew the phone would ring some day and Joshua would be dead." That fear was not unfounded. Two months after the visit, Joshua DeShaney fell into a coma. Emergency room surgeons opened his skull to relieve the pressure on his brain. They found pools of rotted blood from a long period of intercranial bleeding. They also found old bruises all over this body. The boy's life was saved. But loss of half his brain tissue condemned him to permanent paralysis and profound retardation. He is now in a home for the mentally retarded. He cannot walk or talk and has only limited use of his arms.

Appeal to the Courts

Melody DeShaney filed suit in U.S. District Court against the county. Through her attorneys, she claimed that the department's failure to protect her son from his father amounted to a deprivation of liberty in violation of the Fourteenth Amendment. The district court, where the suit was tried, ruled against her. Melody then took the case to a U.S. court of appeals. Her attorneys knew that as a general rule, counties and states are not responsible for ordinary negligence by their employees. But, they argued, "a state can be held to account for failing to act if a `special relationship' exists between the state and the injured party." The court of appeals said, in effect, "That may be, if the injured person is in state custody. But that wasn't the case here. And there is a split of authority as to whether that relationship can exist where he is not in state custody." And that court, too, ruled against the boy.

To the Nation's Highest Court

Was there no "special relationship" between Joshua and the county? Did not the ineffective interviews of police and caseworkers with the DeShaneys create such a relationship? Is there no remedy against a government unit that knows of vicious abuse of a helpless child and sits on its hands?

Melody DeShaney went to the U.S. Supreme Court to find out. By a 6:3 decision, that court decided that there was no such relationship, and that the Fourteenth Amendment did not fasten on the county a duty to protect the child from his father. The Chief Justice wrote, "The state has no constitutional duty to protect Joshua against his father's violence [and] its failure to do so—though calamitous in hindsight—simply does not constitute a violation of the due process clause." He said that because the county had once given Joshua shelter, and because it suspected that he was being abused, was not enough to establish that relationship. "The state does not become the permanent guarantor of an individual's safety by once having offered him shelter," he added. Case dismissed.

What of Randy DeShaney, the reported alcoholic, drug user, and brutalizer of his son? Mr. DeShaney was prosecuted criminally and sentenced to two to four years in jail. In less than two years, he was paroled. He is now free to father more children.

Can We Learn From DeShaney?

Apparently the voluntary counseling given DeShaney had no effect; it may even be that it generated resentments in the father that induced more abuse of the child. What should or could the social services department have done here?

The case was first reported to them by the police. As evidence of abuse piled up, the department could have notified the police of the facts and recommended criminal action against the father. The court could then have put DeShaney on probation, with checkups by the department to continue. At the first sign of further abuse, he would have been rearrested and punished accordingly.

A better approach would have been to obtain a court order removing the child from the abusing parent's custody

правонарушители, преступник

(and finding a suitable home. The order would also require the delinquent parent or parents to attend counseling sessions or other appropriate treatment, with the possibility of the child's being returned if this is successful.

Some states have already enacted legislation designed to give greater protection to children. Perhaps other states, prodded by their citizens and by the DeShaney decision, will improve their laws as well. They should at least authorize their caseworkers and health professionals who might be involved to enter homes with police backup if necessary, inspect premises, question parents, and require production of the child. The child should be carefully examined for indications of physical or sexual abuse, and questioned out of the sight and hearing of parents or custodians. There should also be authorization to question and take statements from neighbors, relatives, or others who may have known about or witnessed child abuse.

But laws cannot help rescue these unfortunate little ones unless someone reports what they cannot report. The reporting can be, and under current laws generally *must* be, reported by health and other professionals who are in contact with such children. There is no other way that we can put serious controls on a most serious human problem.

RELATED ABUSE

Related to, but not part of, physical child abuse is sexual abuse. Since these crimes are usually committed in secret, and because the victims will not, or cannot act for themselves, many of these acts are never detected. Whether there is more of it at present, or more being reported, we cannot know. But figures released by the National Committee for the Prevention of Child Abuse indicate greatly increased annual reports—in some states, more than 100 percent in a single year. In a Kinsey Institute study, the average sexual abuse victim was a girl of 8, with the offense generally involving fondling, heavy petting, exposure, masturbation, and mouth–genital contacts. However, such abuses can occur to children of any age and of either sex. One study estimates that there may be as many as 500,000 cases of abuse a year.

Another estimates that 20 percent of women and 8.6 percent of men have been so abused.

Sexual abuse cases are not physically evident as other forms of abuse may be. They are less likely to be discovered by teachers, ministers, social workers, and so on. Few outside health professionals and their associates, and the parents of molested children, will know of them.

A further secrecy cloak is that many abuses are interfamilial: Parents or relatives or close friends may be involved. Nor will a parent always object to child sexual abuse by the other parent. She or he may hesitate to take action in an effort to preserve a foundering marriage or to provide a continuing home for other children, which might be lost if the family splits.

REPORTING—BOTH LEGAL AND ETHICAL

Where the physician or R.N. discovers or is told about child sexual abuse, it is the person's legal and ethical responsibility to report it. Some may be reluctant to do so, and it may well devolve on you, as an employee in or contractor to their office, to remind them diplomatically.

Two major facts may help you. One is that most physical child abusers (or wife beaters) were themselves victims of abuse as children. It is certainly probable that a child you help rescue from a situation like this would also turn into an abuser. The other fact is a report that 67 percent of San Francisco prostitutes were sexually abused as children. So by reporting a case of physical or sexual child abuse, you may not only be rescuing a victim today but unborn victims of generations to come.

REFERENCES

DeShaney v. Winnebago County, 87-154.

Hurley, Mary M., Duties in Conflict, San Diego Law Review, Vol. 22, p 645.

Kempe, C.H., The Battered Child Syndrome, JAMA, Vol. 17, 1962, p. 181.

Landeros v. Flood, 131 Cal Rptr 73.

MERTENS, ROBERT T., *Child Sexual Abuse, Golden Gate University Law Review*, Vol. 15, p. 437.

Robinson, *Time* November 20, 1972.

San Francisco Chronicle, February 23, 1989.

QUESTIONS

1. A child is brought in by his well-to-do father, who explains that the child, about 6, fell down the stairs. There is a subdural hematoma on the forehead, marks as of strangulation on the throat, and a shoulder dislocation. It is clear to you that the injuries are inconsistent with a fall. Suspecting possible child abuse, you ask the father how the child got that bump on the forehead. The reply, "Must have fallen down stairs; uh huh."

   "When did the fall happen?"

   "Uh, yesterday morning, I think."

   "And when did he dislocate his shoulder?"

   "Well, the same time, I guess."

   "And the marks on his throat?"

   "Well, I don't know about them; maybe when he was playing with the other kids."

   You get the child out of the father's presence and into a treatment room. As soon as you can, you question the child, but cannot get coherent answers.

   You realize that you have no actual proof of child abuse, and that if you err in reporting this as such a case to the authorities, you may become liable. Should you, therefore, report it anyway? Tell the father that you are aware of the abuse and will report him if this happens again? Tell the father that you treated the child only because it was an emergency matter and to take him elsewhere if he is injured again? Explain your answer.

9

Abortion

Does life begin when the ovum is fertilized?

∎

Are abortion laws the same in every state?

∎

Is there a constitutional right to abortion?

∎

What would the effects of a "morning after" pill be?

∎

What changes are taking place in family planning clinics?

Perhaps the most sensitive, painful, and controversial question in all the practice of medicine is the question of abortion. More properly there are several questions. Some cannot be answered by either law or medicine.

THE CRIMINAL VIEW

In has not been many years since abortions were illegal. A pregnant woman or girl could not have her pregnancy terminated by a legitimate physician. There were, however, even in this century, people who set up as back-alley abortionists. Most were far from skilled. Infection was common. A woman going to one of these risked death or butchery at their hands. And the fear, shame, and guilt of going secretly and criminally could add a terrible further burden that she might well carry for the rest of her life.

At the same time, it is probable that medically skillful abortions were being done by legitimate physicians. They did so under laws that permitted abortions where carrying to full term might prove dangerous to the woman's health and well-being. These physicians justified this under the theory that patients might otherwise suffer extreme emotional damage. It was a doubtful theory, but few physicians or their staff were ever prosecuted.

After World War II, American opinion swung in favor of liberalized abortion. Not only individuals, but major organizations such as the American Bar Association, American Medical Association, Association of the University Women, and others lobbied for a change in the laws. Meanwhile, women who could afford to, obtained the services of their personal physicians, or if they could not, went to Japan or Sweden, where the procedure is legal. Many others could not afford those options. We do not know how many tried to abort themselves, or went to unskilled persons, or were forced to bear a child of rape, indiscretion, or where there was simply not enough income for another child.

QUESTION WITHOUT AN ANSWER

Practically everyone has an opinion about abortion, and a great many of us are very vocal on the subject. Antiabortion-

ists want to overturn existing laws and declare abortion illegal again. The details of their beliefs differ: Some think life
begins at the moment of conception and that any attempt to
divert the course of nature then becomes murder. Apparently
this means that a "morning after" pill, taken shortly after
rape, incest, or an abortion needed to save the mother's life,
is also murder.

Others feel that life begins 14 days after the first egg and
sperm unite (the zygote), when the cluster of developed cells
become an embryo. It has no heartbeat, no nervous system,
no brain, or other vital organs. After 55 or so days, rudiments
of organs have appeared. If uninterrupted, the embryo will
become a fetus and in about 273 days will normally become a
human baby.

Most of the controversy seems to center on just when life
begins. Is there truly "life" at the moment of conception? Or
when the embryo develops? Or when organs start? Or at the
moment of birth? Or at some other point? It is pretty well settled that one is dead when the brain no longer functions.
Many people base their opinion on that fact—that one is not
alive until there is a brain to function. This occurs from 24 to
28 weeks after conception.

State laws put different limits on how late in the pregnancy a woman may abort. These limits cluster around the
time at which the fetus may be capable of living outside the
womb.

THE LAW DECIDES

The controversy did not end when, in 1973, the U.S. Supreme
Court held that antiabortion laws were unconstitutional; it
simply changed its objectives. *Roe v. Wade* and *Doe v. Bolton*,
are the two landmark cases. "Jane Roe," brought suit against
the Texas abortion laws. Justice Blackmun wrote the court's
opinion. He said that the Constitution gave us the right of privacy, and this right "is broad enough to encompass a woman's
decision whether or not to terminate her pregnancy." The
court said a fetus is not a "person" entitled to protection under
the Constitution. It did say, however, that the right to abortion
was not unlimited. As long as at least *potential life* of the fetus

is involved, the state may assert interests beyond the protection of the pregnant woman alone, adding that state abortion restrictions can be upheld when they are necessary to protect a compelling state interest.

What would such "compelling interests" be? One would be the state's interest in protecting maternal health and in protecting the human life of the unborn. Because there is less risk early in the pregnancy, the state's interest would arise only when the first trimester had passed: 24 to 28 weeks of gestation. The Texas law was unconstitutional, the split decision said, because it didn't distinguish between early abortions and later ones; also, that the law restricted abortions to cases where they were necessary to save the mother's life and did not include the case where it was necessary to save her health.

The *Roe* decision was clarified in another U.S. Supreme Court case, decided shortly afterward, *Doe v. Bolton.* Here the Court struck down a Georgia law considerably more liberal than that of Texas. That law set up a requirement for abortion review committees in hospitals, mandatory medical consultations and residency requirements. These, the justices said, were regulations that were made to apply throughout the entire pregnancy and the state did not have a compelling interest, at least before the fetus was viable.

DECRIMINALIZING ABORTION

If anything focused American public opinion on the question of abortion, it was the Sherri Finkbine case in 1962. Mrs. Finkbine was pregnant and had been taking the drug thalidomide, developed and used in Europe, where it was considered to be safe and beneficial for expectant mothers. The drug was not generally available in the United States, for the Food and Drug Administration (FDA) had reservations and did not approve it for sale.

The FDA's reservations turned out to be well founded. Thalidomide caused severely deformed fetuses. Fearful that her own fetus had been so affected, Mrs. Finkbine tried to get an abortion in her state, Arizona. She found that at that time, abortions were illegal. She then tried California and New

Jersey, also without success. Finally, she took a highly publicized trip to Sweden, where the procedure was legal. She had her abortion there. Her fears were confirmed; the child, had she carried it to full term, would have been seriously deformed. Most Americans reported in a Gallup Pole—52 percent thought that she was right, 32 percent thought that she was wrong, and the remaining 16 percent had no opinion.

The pot had come to a boil. Three years later, the U.S. Supreme Court ruled that the states had no compelling interest in denying the use of birth control by married couples. They had, the Court said, a right of privacy guaranteed by the U.S. Constitution. Then came the famous *Roe v. Wade* case. The constitutional right to privacy, said the court in its 7:2 decision, includes a woman's right to have an abortion. The court laid down rules concerning the trimesters of pregnancy. The results were clear: abortion on demand.

That was in 1973. The deluge began almost at once. Three years later, the government was funding 350,000 abortions a year—and that didn't include all the women who could afford their own private physicians. By 1976, though, government funding of abortions was severely restricted. Nevertheless, in 1988, 290,000 poor women had the procedure, "paying for it," wrote Susan Terkel in the *Los Angeles Times*, "with money they no doubt could have spent on basics like food and shelter."

AGAIN, THE PENDULUM

The legalization of abortions led to a widespread growth of abortion clinics. Many also gave counsel and advice on the use of birth control methods and provided pelvic examinations, family planning, and related services. Meanwhile, antiabortion groups were becoming active. They lobbied legislatures, demonstrated, and issued literature. The pro-abortion forces were forced to respond.

In Missouri, the legislature passed a law saying that public employees could not use public buildings for abortions, and prohibiting these employees from performing abortions at all except where necessary to save the mother's life. The law was challenged and the case finally reached the U.S.

Supreme Court. By this time there were several new and conservative justices on the bench. On July 3, 1989, they ruled by a 5:4 majority, to uphold parts of the lower court's ruling. That case, *Webster v. Reproductive Health Services*, did not overrule *Roe v. Wade*. It did not say that abortions were once more illegal. It *did* say that each of the fifty states could pass laws requiring physicians to determine at what point a fetus can live outside its mother's womb.

More recently, the high court ruled in another significant abortion case. In *Ada v. Guam*, the justices once again affirmed their earlier ruling in *Roe v. Wade*. The government of Guam passed a law declaring it a *felony* (punishable by at least a year in the penitentiary if guilty) to have an abortion, except in two extreme medical situations. The case went from the trial court to the United States Circuit Court of Appeals. The Court of Appeals said the Guam law was unconstitutional. The government appealed then to the U.S. Supreme Court. Six justices ruled, without comment, that the Court of Appeals was right. Three justices dissented, on technical grounds. They said that although some portions of the Guam law might be unconstitutional, others were not—and should not have been overruled. Nevertheless, the *Roe* decision remains in force, subject to such state restrictions that do not put an undue burden on a woman's right to an abortion.

EFFECT ON MEDICAL PROFESSIONALS

The impact on medical professionals working in family planning, women's health centers, and other areas involved may not be all that pervasive. Patients have been requesting birth control pills to use along with their diaphragms. The idea is that the pills, rather than abortion, would be their backup in case of diaphragm failure.

If you are in any way involved with birth control as a counselor, physician, nurse, or other health worker, you will want to review your state's position on abortion information and consult with your attorney on the effects, if any, of the *Guam* decision. You may also want to be familiar with the laws of other states, particularly those closest to yours, that might have less restrictive requirements, for referral of patients. Also, of course, you will have your directory of clinics that can be most helpful to such patients.

TEENAGE ABORTIONS

Closely related to the abortion problems of adult women are those of girls in their teens who become pregnant. In California alone, a state with 2-1/4 million people, 34,000 teenagers had abortions in a recent year. Some of them became pregnant at 13, 12, and perhaps a few even younger. What are we to do when a child walks into a clinic or medical office and says, "I'd like an abortion, please?" Most likely you'd reply, "Do your parents know about this?" And the youngster replies, "I wouldn't dare tell them; they'd kill me!" Plainly, this young patient needs the guidance and advice of someone far more mature.

On the other hand, doesn't everyone, regardless of age, have a right to privacy and confidentiality? Can you force her to confess to her parents, "Mommy and Daddy, I've done a bad thing?" After the initial shock, most parents would be understanding and supportive. But a few, less stable people might react very badly, possibly driving the child out of the house.

Some states have adopted "squeal laws." One type says that when a teenager applies for an abortion, she must have her parents' consent. The other type says only that they must be notified; consent is not required. Sometimes these laws have bypass provisions. The applicant need not let the parents know but must get approval from a judge. Sometimes, if the abortion is for medical reasons, permission is not required from anyone.

In at least one case that reached the U.S. Supreme Court (*City of Akron v. Akron Center for Reproductive Health*, 1983, 462 US 416), the court struck down a law that required a woman under the age of 15 either to get consent of both parents or a court order. The court said that the law was void because there was no procedure for an individual determination of the young woman's maturity.

More recently, the U.S. Supreme Court reluctantly reviewed *Roe v. Wade*, which declared abortion to be a woman's right. The question was raised by legislation passed in Pennsylvania. This law said that a woman seeking an abortion must give her informed consent beforehand. She must be given specified information at least 24 hours before the procedure. If a minor, she needed the informed consent of at least one parent. If she is married (with some exceptions), she must furnish a signed statement that her husband has been notified.

This latest case, *Planned Parenthood of Southeastern Pennsylvania v. Casey* (1992), retains and reaffirms *Roe v. Wade,* according to Justices O'Connor, Kennedy, and Souter. It does, however, allow the various states to tinker with the concept of legal termination of pregnancies. This is based, it is said, "on the principle that the State has legitimate interests from the outset of the pregnancy in protecting the health of the woman and the life of the fetus that may become a child."

The court recognizes "the right of the woman to choose to have an abortion before viability and to obtain it without undue interference from the State. Before viability, the State's interests are not strong enough to support a prohibition of abortion or the imposition of a substantial obstacle to the woman's effective right to elect the procedure." However, the court confirms "the State's power to restrict abortion after fetal viability, if the law contains exceptions for pregnancies which endanger a woman's life or health."

The heart of the case is the following declaration:

> It is a constitutional liberty of the woman to have some freedom to terminate her pregnancy. We conclude that the basic decision in *Roe* was based on a constitutional analysis which we cannot now repudiate. The woman's liberty is not so unlimited, however, that from the outset the State cannot show its concern for the life of the unborn, and at a later point in fetal development the State's interest in life has sufficient force so that the right of the woman to terminate the pregnancy can be restricted.

The Supreme Court struck down the "husband notification" restriction in the Pennsylvania law. It was declared an "undue burden" and therefore invalid, the Court saying, "A significant number of women will likely be prevented from obtaining an abortion just as surely as if Pennsylvania had outlawed the procedure entirely. The fact that [this law] may affect fewer than one percent of women seeking abortion does not save it from facial invalidity, since the proper focus of constitutional inquiry is the group for whom the law is a restriction, not the group for whom it is irrelevant. [That law] embodies a view of marriage consonant with the common-law status of women but repugnant to this Court's present understanding of marriage and the nature of the rights secured by the Constitution."

The Court said the requirement that a physician give the woman information about the abortion procedure and its risks and alternatives is not an undue burden and not unconstitutional. The decision appeared to leave neither the pro-life adherents nor the freedom of choice groups wholly satisfied. It also left open a number of questions, including federal funding for abortion counseling and appropriate procedures for the conduct of abortion clinics. It is certain that some of these questions will be wending their several ways through the lower courts to definitive decisions.

Ironically, it may be that there is a technological solution to most of the bitter arguments, lawsuits, doubts, split families, and other sequelae of a careless evening. This is a pill, RU-486, now available in France, that aborts the fertilized egg almost immediately on formation. According to reports, it is effective and safe. It is not yet approved for sale in the United States by the Federal Drug Administration. It may never be, due to the political climate.

But one thing is sure. If this new drug—or something similar—is all that it is said to be, American women are going to have it, legally or illegally. This will eliminate the need for surgical procedures that not all of them can afford. It will reduce or stop entirely the psychological trauma that affects many who face the abortion decision. It will give true freedom of choice to women who certainly deserve no less.

QUESTIONS

1. A 15-year-old girl comes to an abortion clinic requesting an abortion. She is well within the first trimester. She explains that while she has been "going with" a boy her own age, the

person really responsible for her pregnancy is a close family member who has been having relations with her for a year. The law in the girl's state requires that at least one parent must be notified. When this is pointed out to the girl, she claims that her parents will be furious: that her mother will side against her in favor of the family member at fault and that she will be thrown out of her home. She has no money and nowhere to go. Which of the following suggestions would be appropriate for the clinic personnel to make?

- Persuade the boy she has been going with (and with whom she has also had relations) that he should marry her
- Notify the district attorney that this constitutes a statutory rape and request criminal action
- Provide her with the requested abortion as requested and without restriction
- Arrange for review by a judge of the courts
- Arrange to send her to another state where there are no restrictions of this kind
- Explain the risk and problems of abortion and suggest that she carry the baby to term

2. A state law requires that a woman seeking an abortion must, at least 24 hours before the procedure, be counseled by a physician or qualified person and be given information about it, including the health risks. She must then give her "informed consent" before the procedure. A situation arises where a woman has given birth to several children, each by a different father. Her condition is such that another pregnancy may endanger her health. However, the woman has severe mental deficiency. She knows what an abortion is, and wants it, but does not appear to fully understand the counseling, and cannot read or understand when read to. In the absence of a meaningful "informed consent," which alternatives would you consider?

- Have her sign a form that indicates that she has been fully informed and furnished printed material and fully understand everything she has heard and read (signing by "X" since she cannot write her name)

- Have a near friend or relative, acting as guardian, sign for her
- Request approval of a court
- Refuse her request since compliance might result in liability for the clinic

10

The Right
to Die

When should life support for a terminally ill patient
be suspended?

∎

Who makes the decision if the patient cannot?

∎

May a patient turn off his or her own life-support
system?

∎

What are the responsibilities of the medical staff for
a brain-dead patient still on life support systems?

∎

When may the medical assistant become involved?

Death comes to us in many ways and in many guises. It may come suddenly, unexpectedly, randomly, as in an airplane crash, an explosion, an accident, or similar means. It may come as a person's own choice of time and means, as in a suicide. But the majority of deaths in the United States are medical in nature, with at least some degree of involvement of physicians and health professionals. At times the medical assistant may play an indirect but important role.

A generation or two ago, the physician with a dying patient could do little to alter the course of death except by morphine to ease the pain. The techniques of medicine have grown enormously in the past few decades. Today, with special equipment and medications, even a brain-dead patient may be kept indefinitely in a semblance of life. For humanitarian reasons, for economic reasons (costs can be thousands of dollars a day), for legal reasons, and for reasons touching on the patient's family, excruciatingly painful decisions must often be made.

In at least one way, the physician's role is exceptionally difficult. He or she is a professional whose entire outlook and philosophy is to nurture life, to heal the patient, to do everything possible to keep the patient alive. For there seems always to be a chance, no matter how removed, that the patient's failing body may somehow rally, and fight, and recover. Would the patient, if he could, want to take that chance? Or, considering the slim odds, would he rather be relieved of his pain, discomfort, dependency, immobility, and fear, and simply go to sleep forever? In a word, when should we pull the plug?

CLASSIC CASE

Karen Ann Quinlan surely had no intimation of the dramatic turn that her life would take when she went to a birthday party with friends on April 14, 1975. In the midst of festivities, the 21-year-old woman suddenly became comatose. She was rushed to a hospital and put on a respirator. Her condition deteriorated. There was a derangement of the cortex of her brain. At times, she sustained loss of breathing—at two different times for as long as 15 minutes. Yet she was not "brain dead" within the usual medical definition. She had no apparent consciousness of those around her. There was a guarded diagnosis that she would never improve, and would die within a year.

Karen's father asked the attending physicians to discontinue her life-support systems. They declined. The father went to court, asking that he be appointed her guardian, with authority to stop all extraordinary medical procedures. Karen's physicians and hospital objected to his appointment; so did the Morris County (New Jersey) prosecutor. Their position was that they could not legally end her support since this would result in her death and might well be considered homicide.

The court did not agree with this viewpoint. The judge granted Karen's father's request for guardianship. He said that it was not homicide for the staff to withdraw life support; death would then be due to natural causes. There is a distinction, he ruled, between unlawfully taking the life of another, and ending the use of artificial life-support systems as a matter of self-determination.

As to the specific circumstances here, the court said that if the physicians and family agreed that there was no chance of recovery, they should consult with the hospital's ethics committee. If the committee agrees that there is no reasonable chance of recovery, support could be withdrawn. The court gave as its opinion that in such a case, there would be no civil or criminal penalties. Other courts and lawyers would agree that penalties would be *unlikely*, but some might feel that the unsettled state of the law does not rule penalties out *completely*.

Ironic Results

Consistent with the New Jersey court's ruling, Karen's systems were withdrawn. According to medical opinion, she should have died very shortly. Instead, Karen was still alive several years later.

Her case, which generated worldwide attention, left many questions unresolved. It did, though, say in effect that Karen (or any other comatose patient) had a right of privacy. That right included her decision to naturally terminate her vegetative existence, and her guardian could assert that right for her, on her behalf. This theory of right of privacy has come up in several cases since then, with differing results.

SINCE QUINLAN

In one case, soon after *Quinlan*, a taxi driver was hospitalized with Lou Gehrig's disease (amyotrophic lateral sclerosis). He was dependent on a respirator and made it clear that he did not want to live in that state. He pulled out his breathing tube; the physicians reinserted it. The patient got his attorney to take the matter to court.

The court ruled that the patient's constitutional right of privacy and self-determination give him the right to turn off the respirator even if it meant he would die, as he intended. The physicians were ordered to turn off the equipment.

Parenthetically, these rights—privacy and self-determination—do not appear in the Constitution in so many words. They evolved by judicial decisions from a First Amendment guarantee of the right of free speech: If I have the right to speak my mind, don't you have an equivalent right not to listen? Obviously, you do; that is your right to privacy—and a right that you can enforce by court action. The courts have applied it in cases of unwanted publicity. You need not have private facts of your life publicly disclosed unless you are a public figure, and not always then. You need not have your photo used commercially without your consent.

As we've seen, the doctrine has been expanded to life-and-death situations such as the landmark *Quinlan* case. Although that case did not speak of a "right to die" in those precise terms, the phrase does come up in current debates on the issue of withdrawal of life supports. Courts and legislatures seem to be enlarging the powers of patients, physicians, and families to make these decisions.

INCURABLE—OR TERMINAL?

Not surprisingly, enlarged powers have enlarged medicolegal problems. The phenomenal advances in medicine have and will continue to alter our present concepts in ways that we cannot conceive. For example, does a competent adult with an incurable illness not yet terminal have the right to disconnect life support systems? In one early case (*Cobbs v. Grant*, 1972) the California Supreme Court ruled that adults of sound mind "can determine whether or not to submit to lawful medical treatment."

But consider the case of William Bartling, 70, who suffered from emphysema, chronic respiratory failure, arteriosclerosis, malignant lung tumor, and an abnormal ballooning of a main artery. He also had a history of alcoholism and was—hardly surprisingly—depressed. He was admitted to the Glendale Adventist Medical Center for treatment of his depression. While he was there, he suffered a collapsed lung. Physicians there put him on a ventilator. Bartling said, "I don't want to be on the ventilator." He was told that he would die if it was removed. He responded, "I don't want to die, either."

They refused to disconnect the equipment and the court was asked to rule on the question. Arguments of the hospital and physicians were to the effect that the patient was incompetent to make a valid decision since he obviously couldn't live without the ventilator; also, that disconnection was suicide if by the patient, and probably homicide if by a staff member.

The court wasn't impressed by any of the arguments. The appellate court ruled that the patient's wish to be free of the ventilator, and yet not die, did not amount to legal incompetence. It said that Bartling's decision took precedence over the hospital's ethical concerns. The disconnection, said the justices, would merely hasten his death by natural causes, not aid his suicide. "Furthermore, in future similar situations, medical people should be free to act according to the patient's instruction without fear of liability and without advance court approval."

INCOMPETENT PATIENTS

What of the gravely ill patient on life support who is unable to communicate his or her wishes because of incompetency?

Must that patient remain on life support indefinitely? Not if while previously competent, he has expressed a wish not to be left a breathing vegetable. Courts have given great weight to that earlier declaration. Provided, the courts say, that there is no reasonable hope of the patient's return to a conscious state, and a bearable state of being, if not recovery.

But the fact is that relatively few people communicate their thought on withdrawal of life support in advance of the event. Where there is no evidence of such an express choice, some courts have allowed life supports to be withdrawn where friends or family said that the patient would have wanted treatment discontinued. Even where the patient had no friends or family, the court considered the patient's condition and made a decision as to what the patient, if competent, would have wanted.

THE NEVER COMPETENT PATIENT

The decisions are difficult enough where the patient was once competent and something is known of his or her attitudes, philosophy, religious beliefs, and social attitudes. What of the patient who was incompetent for at least several years before his life-or-death dilemma?

George Clark was a 45-year-old white male admitted to Cooper Hospital in New Jersey. He had a diagnosis of malnourishment and dehydration; he was unable to eat enough food to keep alive. He had suffered a stroke four years before, resulting in a very low cognitive level. He was not in a coma or vegetative state. The immediate problem was to get adequate nutrition into Mr. Clark. The physicians thought that this could best be accomplished by enterostomy, a procedure in which the nutrition tube was introduced directly into the patient's abdomen, where it could be absorbed most beneficially. However, the procedure was not without some risk.

It was clear that he could live indefinitely if his malnourishment problem were resolved. If it could not be, he would die within a very short time. The questions were, first, was he competent to consent to the surgical procedure himself, and second, if he had the procedure, and it were successful, would his life thereafter be of such value as to be worthwhile or desirable? Quoting an earlier case, the court said that

> the decision-maker must compare the burdens of the patient's life with the treatment to the benefits the patient derives from that life: By this we mean that the patient is suffering, and will continue to suffer throughout the expected duration of his life, unavoidable pain, and that the net burdens of his prolonged life markedly outweigh any physical pleasure, emotional enjoyment, or intellectual satisfaction that the patient may still be able to derive from life. This limited-objective standard permits the termination of treatment for a patient who had not unequivocally expressed his desires before becoming incompetent, when it is clear that the treatment in question *would merely prolong the patient's suffering* (emphasis by the court).

The evidence of physicians and relatives disclosed that Mr. Clark did not appear to be suffering pain, or if he did, it was not recurrent or severe. The enterostomy, if decided upon, would not cause pain other than normal postoperative discomfort. The court also found that

> Clark derives some benefits from life. He is able to interact with his environment and to purposefully attempt to communicate. In response to Dr. Wolfson's question of whether he was happy, Clark stated "Yes. He also answered "Yes" on two separate occasions when asked if he was hungry and if he wanted food. It is clear that Clark feels hunger and thirst. Further, Dr. Spence observed that Clark seemed to enjoy eating ice cream during the doctor's visit...[suggesting] that he derives pleasure from tasting certain types of food. Finally, although Clark's cognitive level is low, he seems to derive some emotional and intellectual pleasure from life.

The court considered an objective test for circumstances of this kind:

1. The net burdens of the patient's life with the treatment should clearly and markedly outweigh the benefits that the patient derives from life.
2. The recurring, unavoidable, and severe pain of the patient's life with the treatment should be such that the

effect of administering life-sustaining treatment would be inhumane.

The court then decided that the net burdens of Clark's life with the enterostomy do not markedly outweigh the benefits that he derives from life. Administering this type of treatment is not inhumane, since it would not cause or prolong suffering for Clark. It was therefore in his interests to undergo the enterostomy procedure. The procedure was done. There were complications caused by the subclavian catheter used to nourish him, but these were cleared and he was discharged from Cooper in about three weeks and returned to Lakeland Hospital, where he was able to receive continuing care.

BRAIN-DEAD PATIENTS

The courts have generally found little difficulty in ordering the removal of life-support systems, even over the opposition of relatives, where physicians can testify that the patient shows little, if any, electrical activity in the brain. Thus in the *Dority* case, parents who were suspected of being responsible for an infant's injuries refused consent to withdrawal of a respirator that maintained the child's bodily functions. The court ruled that once brain death was determined by a proper medical diagnosis or by a court, medical personnel would not be liable, civilly or criminally, for disconnecting life-sustaining devices.

Another court came to a similar decision in similar circumstances. Parents who had apparently been responsible for a 17-month-old child's injury opposed withdrawal of its life-support system. In *Lovato*, on finding that the child had suffered brain death, the court ordered the child's guardians to execute a document authorizing the treating physician and hospital to remove all life-support devices.

Where another patient was in a deep coma, the court (re: *Jones*) heard testimony from the treating physician, the hospital review committee, and two physicians appointed by the court. They said that the patient was brain dead, that the condition was permanent and irreversible, and that it was no longer appropriate to maintain life support. The court allowed discontinuance of that support.

BEGINNINGS OF GUIDELINES

There are the beginnings of some guidelines for medical professionals in some of these painful and difficult decisions. One state—California—has passed the Natural Death Act (Health and Safety Code 7185-7195). This states that "adult persons have the fundamental right to control the decisions relating to the rendering of their own medical care, including the decision to have life-sustaining procedures withdrawn or withheld in instances of terminal condition."

The President's Commission for the Study of Ethical Problems in Medicine and Biomedical and Behavioral Research approves of this reasoning. Its report states that a patient may decide to forgo burdensome treatment when it is unlikely that his or her condition will significantly improve.

WHEN DIRECTIVES WOULD HELP

Prospective patients can sometimes save their families and medical professionals enormous difficulties and anguish if they will express their wishes before the need for decision arises. They can state in a simple written letter, or verbally to at least two close relatives or friends, that they do or do not want to remain on life-support systems if their case is hopeless, or they cannot be returned to a reasonably tolerable state of health. Their own physician may be able to furnish an appropriate form. Ideally, they might consult an attorney. But their own expression of wishes, if clear and unambiguous, should be sufficient.

A patient who fails to do this can create extremely severe problems for those who care for her. Such as a charge of murder against her physicians. This actually occurred in *Barber v. Superior Court,* 1983. Clarence Herbert, 55, knew that his operation was risky; he said that he wanted to be kept off life-support machines. Following the planned surgery, Mr. Herbert slipped into an irreversible coma. The medical staff put him on a ventilator and feeding tubes. His family, knowing his wishes, asked that the support systems be disconnected. The physicians agreed; the patient died six days later.

The district attorney's office then filed murder charges against the two treating physicians on the grounds that they had deliberately reduced his life span by removing life-sustaining equipment. The appellate court dismissed the charges. The justices said that the patient's own desires should guide the surrogate decision maker and that if the patient's choice cannot be ascertained, the patient's best interests should guide the surrogate. "Under this standard, such factors as the relief of suffering, the preservation or restoration of functioning and the quality as well as the extent of life sustained may be considered," the court said. The court mentioned the lack of statute law on the subject and said that the physicians could rely on instructions from the patient's family or other available next of kin, consistent with the presidential commission's recommendations.

BASIC ETHICAL PROBLEM

A number of bioethical committees have formulated guidelines to help these life-and-death decision makers. For example, a joint committee of the Los Angeles County Bar and Medical Associations have been working on guidelines to help resolve some of the problems. Bioethical committees attached to health care institutions are often called upon to review decisions made by patients, families, and physicians. Their work varies, but in the main, they review prognoses and serve as forums for the discussion of ethical and social concerns.

There is hope that some nonjudicial review organization can assume the responsibility for these grave decisions. Most legal and health professionals agree that going to court in times of extreme familial emotion is an added stress and places an additional burden on the patient and family. More than twenty states have already passed, or are considering "right to die" laws, and no doubt there will be more.

VALUABLE STAFF HELP

Unless you are a physician, you will not as a staff member make decisions regarding suspension of life support. However, such a decision is a very personal matter, and there may well be times when patients will turn to you for "unofficial" advice or support. Or you may be a listener to the physician's concerns. Compassion and understanding of the family's feelings are important as well as a grasp of the discussion here. Listening to the patient and communicating his or her feelings to the physician can be an extremely important function.

Do not attempt to assume the responsibility yourself. Where there are situations or questions that you or your colleagues cannot handle, there are several types of help available. Among them are bioethical committees, medical societies, hospital chaplains, social workers, lawyers, and hospital ethics committees.

Where possible, there should be discussions with the patient and family before the need for a decision arises. Understanding and agreement in advance can help alleviate possible guilt feelings of family members or to face an eventuality that they may have been avoiding. An amicable, supportive family can do much to ease the patient's anxiety, distress, and pain both for the patient and for his or her loved ones. You will be doing the highest form of health service to help them achieve such a state of mind.

QUESTIONS

1. A man's wife of forty years is on life-support systems. Although heavily sedated, she appears to be in considerable pain. There is no question of her survival for more than a week or two. The man is greatly disturbed. He asks that the life-support system be terminated. The physicians tell him that in this state, withdrawal could be held tantamount to homicide. Without some expression from the patient herself, they cannot do as he requests. Late that night the man is at the wife's bedside. A student nurse comes in to check on the patient.

   The man says, "Look, miss, I want you to do me an important favor. I'm giving you these ten $100 bills for the favor. All you need to do is to come back in an hour and reconnect this equipment, which I intend to stop. By that time, she'll be dead. God rest her...."

The nurse is sure that the dying patient would approve of her husband's act. Would it be professionally wrong for her to do as requested? Would it be wrong if she took the money for doing it? Would the fact that some states have approved "plug-pulling" under similar circumstances justify her act?

2. A patient has inoperable cancer and is deteriorating. He knows that he is terminal, with only a few weeks at most. His physician is a friend with whom he has frequently played golf and tennis. The patient says, "Fred, I don't want to go through this stupid wasting-away, painful agony over a long period of time. Promise me that when the pain really begins, you'll slip an overdose of morphine into me."

The physician sadly refuses.

"Thought you might not. That's okay. I don't blame you. But I haven't been sleeping well lately. Why don't you prescribe a supply of phenobarbitol for me?"

The physician understands that his friend will use the tablets to commit suicide.

- Should he prescribe the phenobarbitol?
- Should he warn the patient's family of the patient's intentions?
- Should he consider that the patient could very well, without his participation, end his life with a gun or other means?
- Would prescribing a legitimate drug for an illegal act be a criminal act as well as grounds for medical discipline?

What reasons might the physician give for the patient not taking his own life but awaiting death by natural means?

11

AIDS and the Medical Worker

May a prospective employer ask that you take an AIDS antibody test as part of your preemployment physical examination?

∎

Are you at risk in handling the blood or other bodily fluids of an AIDS patient?

∎

What are your chances of getting AIDS if you are accidentally stuck with a needle used on a patient with AIDS?

∎

What is the physician's duty to the AIDS patient when all therapies have been tried and are no longer effective?

A NEW BLACK DEATH

Devastating plagues are nothing new in the world's history. There was one in the time of Moses, when a plague—probably bubonic—was visited on the Egyptians. In the second century A.D., Rufus of Ephesus, a physician, wrote of pestilential buboes in Libya, Egypt, and Syria. There was another great cycle in Europe in the sixth century. Then a wave came down out of China in 1348, rolling over Europe and wiping out people by the tens of thousands. Probably a third of what we now call the Western world died of the Black Death. We now have bubonic plague pretty well under control, although a few cases occasionally pop up. But even before its virtual eradication, people did recover, particularly the physically well conditioned and well nourished.

Today we must cope with an even more deadly and relentless killer. Acquired immunodeficiency syndrome (AIDS) leaves few, if any, survivors. How long it has existed no one knows. It surfaced in 1981 when a cluster of homosexual men were discovered with an unknown, fatal infection. In less than three years, researchers tagged the virus that caused people's immune systems to fail so that they could no longer fight off various serious illnesses. By the time they did so, 12,000 Americans had become victims, and many more were active carriers. Today, backed in part by the federal government, there has been progress in the counterattack. Several agents have been developed that at least prolong lives, and there is promise of even more effective therapies.

The true malevolence of AIDS is not merely that it is a sexually transmitted disease. Syphilis and gonorrhea are sexual transmitted diseases, too, but they become known to the patient rather quickly and can be treated successfully. Thus the exposure time for infecting others is relatively short. The AIDS virus, on the other hand, may remain dormant for years, while the patient-to-be unwittingly infects a whole string of other persons, who in turn infect many others.

It is conceivable that if AIDS had begun a generation or two ago, before the development of virology, the entire world population, directly or indirectly, might have been wiped out. As it is, we know how to slow its progress, and a great many people are changing their lifestyles to reduce their risk. Another major source of infection is the use of dirty needles by drug users. This impact could be greatly reduced by the simple expedient of furnishing habitual drug users with sterile, disposable needles.

ON-THE-JOB PROTECTION

As a health worker, your risk of catching any infectious disease depends to a great extent on how close you must work with patients having infectious diseases. Plainly those who have direct care of patients, such as physicians, nurses, nurses aids, and medical technicians have a degree of risk. But in every disease, including AIDS, the risk can be well controlled.

If you're a medical librarian, medical transcriber, secretary, office manager, or clerk, you are seldom in contact with patients, so any risk is practically nonexistent. Of course, like the general population, you may pick up an airborne virus, such as colds or flu—but not AIDS. The main routes of the AIDS virus into the body are transmission through sexual relations, contaminated hypodermic needles, or other transmission of blood or bodily secretions.

Some of the stories recently in circulation about the ease of AIDS contagion are greatly exaggerated, and some are completely false. There are no reported cases of the disease being transmitted by mosquitoes or other insects. Bites by struggling criminals or mental patients who have the virus have not resulted in the bitten persons becoming infected.

Accidental sticking with a needle is not uncommon among technicians, nurses, and some other health workers. There has been fear that a worker could thus become infected. This fear, too, has thus far proved unfounded. A group of 666 people who had sustained needle-sticks were checked. Only 1.7 percent were antibody positive, and all but three of these were high-risk people who might already have been infected. In those three, the source of infection could not be determined. In another group of 105 stuck accidentally with needles used on AIDS patients, none tested positive after eight months. Given the long incubation period of AIDS, this is not conclusive but indicates that the risk is very slight.

If you are working with patients who may have AIDS, you will probably be required to use the same precautions that you would use for other blood-transmissible diseases, such as hepatitis B. You should wear gloves and take care to cover any portions of your skin that may be broken. Wash carefully after handling the patient, and follow hospital or clinic guidelines for disposing of used needles, bodily fluids, or other waste products from the patient.

There has been some concern as to whether you, as a health worker, have a legal right to require a patient to be tested for AIDS if you are accidentally stuck with a needle used on him or her. As mentioned, there seems only a remote possibility that you would be infected. In at least two states you cannot, by statute, force anyone to be tested or to reveal information. There is litigation pending as to whether a health care worker who has had direct contact, or a needle-stick, has this right.

It seems probable that the eventual court decision will be against the testing because (1) the chance of infection appears to be so remote, and (2) there is strong sentiment for preserving the person's privacy.

HIRING AND FIRING

Marna J. is a skilled medical secretary who works primarily for Dr. Fosler, chief of the urology department. For some time, Dr. Fosler has been aware of rumors about Marna. She is said to have AIDS and some of the workers have become nervous about the situation. Morale is definitely affected.

Finally, Dr. Fosler realizes that he must take a stand. "Marna," he says, "I'm sorry to have to bring this up, but there seems to be a general impression around here that you have AIDS. Is it true?"

Marna nods. "But I can work all right. You're satisfied with what I'm doing, aren't you?"

"Very much so. You're still the best medical secretary I ever had. I'm afraid, though, that there's a serious problem with others on the staff. I've received several notes—some anonymous—that you should be transferred or discharged."

Marna says, "But I need to work! Treatment is expensive, even with insurance. And I need to save something, too—for later...."

Dr. Fosler's dilemma is a cruel one. But it is not insoluble. The hospital receives federal funds for Medicare and other services. This brings it under the federal Vocational Rehabilitation Act of 1973. This pre-AIDS law says that such employers cannot refuse to hire, or to retain handicapped employees, unless the handicap substantially interferes with the employee's "ability to perform essential job functions with reasonable accommodation, or when the handicap poses a substantial possibility of harm to others."

So when is a person handicapped? The act doesn't say. But in 1987 a case went to the U.S. Supreme Court that was significant. It ruled on a case involving a teacher who had tuberculosis, a contagious disease. Such a person was a handicapped person of the kind protected by the act. The employer had argued that even a handicapped person can be discharged if other employees are fearful—although mistakenly so—of the possible contagion. The Court met this argument. It said, "[S]ociety's accumulated myths and fears can well be replaced by reasoned and medically sound judgments." This case (School Board of Nassau County v. Arline, March 3, 1987 55 USLW 4245) seems to cover Dr. Fosler's situation. The only way a fellow worker could catch AIDS from Marna would be through sexual contact—not a very likely possibility, since everyone around had head of her affliction.

Legally, the hospital must retain Marna as long as she is reasonably capable of doing her job. But what of the frightened staff? Some employers have wisely begun low-key educational programs designed to quiet the panic through factual information. The effectiveness seems to be higher where there is a health and safety education program, including memos or newsletters with a mix of health information and AIDS knowledge. This can be enhanced if it is possible to attribute the information to a well-known local physician.

Note, however, that so far we have been talking about *federal* law. The Vocational Rehabilitation Act applies to workers in government hospitals and other government facilities. What about workers in the various states? Are they covered under state law?

Discrimination Strongly Discouraged

Theoretically, some state courts might come to a conclusion contrary to that of the U.S. Supreme Court in the *Arline* case, but this is rather unlikely. Many states have antidiscrimination laws. They cover AIDS in a general way, treating the disease as a "covered handicap." A recent study (National Gay Rights Advocates, *A Survey of the Fifty States...*, 1986) showed that two-thirds of the fifty states are willing to accept complaints based on AIDS discrimination.

Although employers risk damage suits by discrimination because of AIDS, they need not accept substantially less than reasonable work performance. If the illness forces a great deal of absenteeism, or if the infected person is unable to perform with reasonable satisfaction, the law is flexible. The employer would have three alternatives. One would be to transfer the person to another department or job, where with some assistance, he or she could carry on in an acceptable fashion. Another would be to place the person on involuntary medical leave. And a third (provided that all steps taken by the employer have been carefully documented) would be termination.

Medical Screening

How does a medical worker handle the problem of pre- or postemployment testing for AIDS? A few states have already passed laws prohibiting the use of blood tests to detect the virus. Others may come to the same conclusion through the general prohibition in their laws of handicap discrimination.

In effect, the employer may only ask the reasonable question, "Do you now have a medical condition that might interfere with your ability to do the job for which you have applied?" A person may be HIV-positive and never come down with AIDS. Or he or she may be in the early stages of AIDS and able to work indefinitely. Such workers might truthfully answer "no" in either case.

The person in a more advanced state of the disease has a more difficult ethical problem. He or she may have recovered from an AIDS-related pneumonia or cancer and may feel that new medical discoveries and treatment may keep him from further ailments for the foreseeable future. In that case, his or her answer will be in accordance with that belief.

INSURANCE WHEN THE CHIPS ARE DOWN

A lot of people buy fire insurance on their homes. But only a very small percentage ever have fires. When one does, the insurance company pays for the fire damage, which can be in the hundreds of thousands of dollars. The company pays it out of funds that it has collected from all those other home-owners. This is the principle of "spreading the risk."

The same principle is used in health insurance, although certainly in a more complex fashion; everyone pays, but not everyone gets sick—or not very, or not often. Some of us do get very sick and require expensive treatment, often over a long period of time. Obviously, the health insurance companies aren't eager to cover people who are likely to become expensive. So many insurance executives want to exclude experimental treatments for AIDS. Since a great deal of treatment at this point in research is experimental, these executives would only pay a portion, if anything, of most forms of treatments.

Some insurers also want to use the HIV test for applicants, as a measure of insurability. The problem here is that a person may be HIV-positive and never come down with AIDS. A significant proportion do—and the companies would just as soon not write policies for them. The laws, like the opinions, are diverse at present.

Is HIV testing a "discriminatory practice"? Insurers say no, that in a sense they have always "discriminated"—that is, most applicants are medically tested. If, for example, they have cancer, or a bad heart, or a bad back, treatment for those conditions may be excluded. However, the company might agree to cover other conditions that the applicant does not yet (and may never) have. Nevertheless, it has been pointed out that unlike their practice in other types of diseases, the insurers are not using broad-based actuarial data. In other words, they are not using the known odds that an applicant will or will not develop AIDS.

It is not only the health insurance, but the life insurance companies too, that have problems connected with AIDS. Let's say that a young man in a high-risk group is privately tested and discovers that he is HIV-positive. He realizes that if AIDS develops, his life expectancy is only a few years. He wants to provide for his loved ones. So he applies for life insurance. Is it ethical for him to state in his application that he has no communicable diseases? Does the insurance company have a right to test applicants to check the facts for themselves?

Insurance companies report an upsurge in the amounts of life insurance that some young people are applying for. This will typically be four or five times the average amounts sought by other young people in the same age group. The companies are generally of the opinion that these high-figure applicants are very likely suffering from AIDS, or are HIV-positive and believe that their lives are severely limited.

There is danger here. If the company does not know and has not been told of the applicant's condition, it may, in the event of his death, refuse payment. This would be on the grounds of concealment of a material fact. Of course, if the person took out his insurance policy *before* he knew that he was seropositive, the company has no legitimate complaint and must pay the full amount of the policy to the beneficiaries.

One Canadian company recently decided that they would, if the insured person so requested and was definitely terminal, advance a substantial part of the face amount to *him*, rather than his beneficiary, with the salutary thought that he probably had much greater need than the named beneficiary. Of course, this is predicated on the policy having been taken out before the insured person acquired his illness. Some other insurers have announced similar policies since then.

DUTY OF MEDICAL PROFESSIONALS

Is a medical professional legally bound to treat an AIDS patient who seeks his or her services? Here the term *medical professional* includes nurses, physicians, various technicians, medical assistants, ambulance drivers, paramedics, and others. For centuries the law has been that these professionals are not compelled to treat anyone who comes to them. The relationship between them and the patients was considered to be a matter of private contract: *I will do this for you* (diagnose and treat) *if you will do that for me* (you or your insurer will pay for the services). Neither party, the law said, has the right to force the relationship on the other. For good reason: A patient or physician coerced or forced into the relationship will not have the confidence, trust, or faith so essential to rapid recovery.

But despite this freedom from compulsion, there has been strong *moral* pressure to treat anyone in distress. There are hundreds of examples of medical professionals risking their own lives to save others at the battle front, in parachuting into inaccessible areas to treat injured hunters or hikers, and in treating people with highly contagious diseases. The American Medical Association's Code of Ethics states that a physician in an emergency should render service to the best of his ability. Note they say "should," not "must." Thus at least until the last few years, the medical professional was as free to choose or not choose patients as the patients were to choose or not choose the professional. But now, after centuries, the tide seems about to turn.

CASE READY TO BE MADE

It may be that at this very moment an AIDS patient is applying to a medical professional for help and is being told that he cannot be accepted as a patient. And it may be that the patient, humiliated, desperate, frightened, and filled with rage, goes to an attorney. "I've got insurance," he says, "and I've got money, and I'm a steady, responsible person. He *ought* to take me, and I want to see him pay damages before I die. Maybe it'll teach him a little more humanity."

The attorney tells him, "If you had ever been a patient of his, Mr. Kenworthy, you might have a good case. Perhaps on the basis of his abandonment of you."

Kenworthy says, "I've never been his patient. But I've heard he's a very fine physician."

"Well, as far as I know, no appeals court has held squarely on the nose that a health professional has a legal duty to treat everyone who walks in the door. However, there seems to be a real movement in that direction. For one thing, the lawmakers have been encouraging medical professionals to help out in emergency situations by passing Good Samaritan laws. Those laws protect them from being sued later for malpractice unless they were grossly negligent. A few states do require treatment in emergency situations, but only if the physician was at the scene of the accident when it happened."

Some cities have laws that prohibit discrimination against AIDS victims. Doctors and dentists in those cities may not refuse treatment to anyone who has an AIDS-related complex (ARC), who has the virus, or who is even *thought* to have AIDS. As yet, these laws cover only a very small part of our total population. But they appear to be well thought out and will very likely be adopted by more and more cities and states.

It is not clear that these laws apply to *all* doctors and dentists. What if an AIDS patient seeks out a practitioner who, we'll say, is an ophthalmologist and has little or no experience in the field of AIDS? This eye doctor declines to treat on the basis of his lack of knowledge. Has he or she broken the law? Probably not. As long as the refusal to treat is because of inexperience *and not because the person has AIDS*, the law would not apply.

MAY HOSPITALS REFUSE?

Hospitals are in a different category from that of individual physicians or other health professionals. A hospital that receives federal funds may be risking loss of those funds for refusal to treat AIDS patients. The problem is acute, since hospital care for a patient with AIDS is considerably more expensive than for patients with other terminal diseases.

Health professionals who are employees of a hospital, contrary to independent practitioners, are required to provide their particular skills to anyone the hospital admits. That applies to physicians, nurses, technicians, and all other health professionals. The rule is that as employees receiving compensation for their work, they have an obligation to care for anyone assigned to them. If they choose not to do so, they may request deferral of the assignment, or they may resign—or be discharged.

Private, as contrasted with public hospitals generally do have the right to decline patients. But declining is not considered ethical behavior. Moreover, such a right as they do have is rapidly eroding. Under some state laws, they may be considered "places of public accommodation," such as hotels, buses, places of amusement, and so on. As such, they could be liable to heavy damages and penalties under state antidiscrimination law. They also risk losing their tax status as charitable organizations.

It is understandable that people should fear this truly dreadful disease. That fear has already affected the lives of millions of us. Many who had been sexually active have changed and restricted themselves to one companion. But some will be torn by their memories, for AIDS has a very long incubation period. *What about Charlie, six years ago, before I was married? Was that girl I met in Las Vegas okay? Why didn't I use a condom? What a klutz I was, shooting it up back then in my don't-give-a-damn period. That needle—everyone was using it....*

The health professional knows now that all too many people have reason to be fearful. But being professionals, there is much that can be done to counsel and help them.

1. *Suggest an HIV test.* If the results are positive, recommend possible administration of AZT, now proved to effectively retard development of the AIDS virus.
2. *Explain the techniques of safe sex.* Couples need not go loveless out of fear. There are several satisfying sexual activities that will not transmit the virus.
3. *Explain how to clean a needle or syringe.* A thorough cleansing with 40 percent alcohol or 10 percent household bleach (one part bleach, nine parts water) will make it safe.
4. *Recommend the use of a condom and spermicide.* This is the subject of a strong national campaign. Use condoms if not 100 percent sure of both parties.

5. *Stress that no one gets AIDS through casual contact.* Without a mingling of blood or semen, the vicious little virus is not communicable.

QUESTIONS

1. After she graduated from medical school and obtained her degree, Martha Blaney went directly into research work, for which she had a considerable talent. She has been with an ethical pharmaceutical company for eleven years and has become a vice president of the firm.

A neighbor, Stella Wyant, stops by Dr. Blaney's home one evening. She is, the doctor perceives, on the verge of hysteria. "Martha," she says, "I've got AIDS. Must have been four years ago. Charley and I had a big fight and I got involved with this guy...anyway, Charley and I made up. He'd kill me if he knew that I'd been playing around on him. You've got to help me. I don't dare go to our regular doctor—he'd let it slip to Charley."

Uncomfortably, Dr. Blaney says, "Stella, I understand, and I sympathize with you greatly. But I'm not in medical practice. I'm a researcher. I don't know any more about AIDS than I do about what makes my car go. Surely you can find a physician who...."

"No, no! I can't go to a stranger with something like this. Help me, please, Martha."

"I'm truly sorry, Stella. I'm simply not qualified to help you. It would be unethical for me to take on a case for something I know almost nothing about."

Stella goes into a rage. "It's unethical for you to refuse to help me, too! And I'll fix you for this! I'm seeing a lawyer tomorrow!"

There is no specific law in Stella's state saying that a physician must take any patient who walks in the door. But there is a case holding that where a physician refused to treat a patient for racial reasons, he can be held liable. This was under a law that made a refusal to furnish goods or services because of race, religion, sex, or national origins an act of discrimination.

Was Dr. Blaney discriminating against her friend? Should the holder of a medical degree be required to treat anyone who asks, regardless of qualifications, once told of that lack? If Stella carries out her threat to sue, what arguments might be made by attorneys on either side of the case? Good Samaritan laws protect medical personnel who give medical services in emergency situations. Would such a law apply here?

Index

license revocation; must
specify grounds, 58
seldom lost forever, 56
Licensing boards:
peer reviews, 47
sworn testimony, 47

M

Malpractice:
insurance against, 48
late discovery of, 26
minors' rights, 26
reducing risks, 73–75
Malpractice insurance:
where to get it, 71–72
Medical assistants:
may not inform patients, 10
pre-op role, 5
Mentally impaired patients:
informing, 4

P

Patient confidentiality:
asbestosis, 78–79
disability information, 78
waived in workers compensation cases, 78
Patient request, 8
Privilege:
as defense to defamation, 45–46
Professional judgment, 4
Professional liability (See malpractice):
liability for employee acts, 63
reasonable and ordinary skill sufficient, 64
risk exposure, 62
zero defects expectations, 63
Property damage:
patients' property, 66

Q

Quinlan (Karen Ann) case:
right to die, 110–12

R

Registered nurses, State Board of:
complaint against nurse, 53
diagnosing as violation, 53
Release:
of physician and hospital, 6
reminding physician, 6
Responsibility:
level of training, 3
Revocation of license:
by disciplinary board, 56
Religious objection to procedure, 10
Right to die:
extraordinary medical procedures, 111
listen to patient, 119
many states have passed laws, 118
right to privacy, 111
staff help, 119
when to pull the plug, 110
Risks:
failure to warn patient fully, 4
who tells patient?, 3

S

Staff reduction:
dangers of, 32
documenting errors, 33
Slip and fall cases:
all levels sued, 66
Standard of care:
injury resulting from treatment, 64

physician-patient relationship, 63
Statute of limitations:
  chart, file destruction, 69
  same as "outlawing," 68
  starts to run, 69–70
  subpoenas, 69
Subpoenas:
  court appearances, 80
  duces tecum, 79
  must respond to, 79
  to take deposition, 80
Supervisors:
  reasonable rules for, 36
Summons:
  "declarations," "complaints,"
    "petitions," 80

T

Termination:
  counselling employee, 59
  documentation, 59
  recording employee perfor-
    mance, 48
  note keeping, 59
  wrongful, 59

U

Unqualified health workers:
  brain damage by, 32
  treatment by, 31
Unprofessional conduct:
  disciplinary boards, 56

V

Violations, unintentional, 57

W

Witnesses:
  answers, 47
  overanswering, 47
Witnesses, good:
  attitude, 85
  appearance and manners,
    83
  documenting answers, 47
  facts versus opinions, 84
  dressing for hearing, 81
Written consent:
  when needed, 3